eKNOW 2017

The Ninth International Conference on Information, Process, and Knowledge Management

March 19 – 23, 2017

Nice, France

eKNOW 2017 Editors

László Grad-Gyenge, Creo Group, Hungary
Roy Oberhauser, Aalen University, Germany

Printed from e-media with permission by:

Curran Associates, Inc.
57 Morehouse Lane
Red Hook, NY 12571

Some format issues inherent in the e-media version may also appear in this print version.

Printed by Curran Associates, Inc. (2017)

International Academy, Research, and Industry Association (IARIA)
412 Derby Way
Wilmington, DE 19810

Phone: (408) 893-6407
Fax: (408) 527-6351

petre@iaria.org

Additional copies of this publication are available from:

Curran Associates, Inc.
57 Morehouse Lane
Red Hook, NY 12571 USA
Phone: 845-758-0400
Fax: 845-758-2633
Email: curran@proceedings.com
Web: www.proceedings.com

Table of Contents

eKNOW 2017

Forward

The ninth edition of the International Conference on Information, Process, and Knowledge Management (eKNOW 2017) was held in Nice, France, March 19 - 23, 2017. The event was driven by the complexity of the current systems, the diversity of the data, and the challenges for mental representation and understanding of environmental structure and behavior.

Capturing, representing, and manipulating knowledge was and still is a fascinating and extremely useful challenge from both theoretical and practical perspective. Using validated knowledge for information and process management and for decision support mechanisms raised a series of questions the eKNOW 2017 conference was aimed at.

eKNOW 2017 provided a forum where researchers were able to present recent research results and new research problems and directions related to them. The topics covered aspects from knowledge fundamentals to more specialized topics such as process analysis and modeling, management systems, semantics processing and ontology.

We take this opportunity to thank all the members of the eKNOW 2017 Technical Program Committee as well as the numerous reviewers. The creation of such a broad and high-quality conference program would not have been possible without their involvement. We also kindly thank all the authors who dedicated much of their time and efforts to contribute to the eKNOW 2017. We truly believe that, thanks to all these efforts, the final conference program consists of top quality contributions.

This event could also not have been a reality without the support of many individuals, organizations, and sponsors. We are grateful to the members of the eKNOW 2017 organizing committee for their help in handling the logistics and for their work to make this professional meeting a success.

We hope that eKNOW 2017 was a successful international forum for the exchange of ideas and results between academia and industry and for the promotion of progress in knowledge management research.

We also hope that Nice provided a pleasant environment during the conference and everyone saved some time for exploring this beautiful city.

eKNOW 2017 Chairs

eKNOW Steering Committee

Roy Oberhauser, Aalen University, Germany
Conceição Granja, Norwegian Centre for eHealth Research | University Hospital of North Norway, Norway
Andrzej M.J. Skulimowski, AGH University of Science and Technology - Krakow, Poland
Dirk Malzahn, Dirk Malzahn Ltd. / HfH University, Germany
Peter Bellström, Karlstad University, Sweden
Susan Gauch, University of Arkansas, USA
Edy Portmann, Institute of Information Systems - University of Bern, Switzerland
Nitin Agarwal, University of Arkansas at Little Rock, USA

eKNOW Industry/Research Advisory Committee

Gil Ad Ariely, Interdisciplinary Center Herzliya (IDC), Israel
Daniel Kimmig, solute GmbH, Germany
Mauro Dragoni, Fondazione Bruno Kessler, Italy
Dayu Yuan, Google Inc., USA
Ming Zhou, Microsoft Research Asia, China

eKNOW 2017

COMMITTEE

eKNOW Steering Committee

Roy Oberhauser, Aalen University, Germany
Conceição Granja, Norwegian Centre for eHealth Research | University Hospital of North Norway, Norway
Andrzej M.J. Skulimowski, AGH University of Science and Technology - Krakow, Poland
Dirk Malzahn, Dirk Malzahn Ltd. / HfH University, Germany
Peter Bellström, Karlstad University, Sweden
Susan Gauch, University of Arkansas, USA
Edy Portmann, Institute of Information Systems - University of Bern, Switzerland
Nitin Agarwal, University of Arkansas at Little Rock, USA

eKNOW Industry/Research Advisory Committee

Gil Ad Ariely, Interdisciplinary Center Herzliya (IDC), Israel
Daniel Kimmig, solute GmbH, Germany
Mauro Dragoni, Fondazione Bruno Kessler, Italy
Dayu Yuan, Google Inc., USA
Ming Zhou, Microsoft Research Asia, China

eKNOW 2017 Technical Program Committee

Gil Ad Ariely, Interdisciplinary Center Herzliya (IDC), Israel
Chris Adetunji, University of Southampton, UK
Nitin Agarwal, University of Arkansas at Little Rock, USA
Zbigniew Banaszak, Koszalin University of Technology, Poland
Gianni Barlacchi, University of Trento, Italy
Peter Bellström, Karlstad University, Sweden
Martine Cadot, LORIA - University Henri Poincaré Nancy I, France
Ali Çakmak, Istanbul Sehir University, Turkey
Enrico Caldarola, Università di Napoli "Federico II", Italy
Ricardo Campos, Polytechnic Institute of Tomar / LIAAD INESC TEC, Portugal
Massimiliano Caramia, University of Rome "Tor Vergata", Italy
Shayok Chakraborty, Arizona State University, USA
Dickson Chiu, The University of Hong Kong, Hong Kong
Ritesh Chugh, Central Queensland University, Australia
Paolo Cintia, University of Pisa / KDDLab Isti Cnr, Italy
Marco Cococcioni, University of Pisa, Italy
Chiara Di Francescomarino, Fondazione Bruno Kessler (FBK), Italy
Giuseppe A. Di Lucca, University of Sannio - RCOST (Research Center on Software Technology), Italy
Mauro Dragoni, Fondazione Bruno Kessler, Italy
Schaumlechner Erwin, Tiscover GmbH, Austria
Joan-Francesc Fondevila-Gascón, UPF | Blanquerna-URL | UdG (Escola Universitària Mediterrani) | UCJC, UOC, UAB & UB | CECABLE, Spain
Susan Gauch, University of Arkansas, USA

Copyright Information

An Economic Approach to Business Rules Normalization

Martijn Zoet
Optimizing Knowledge-Intensive Business Processes
Zuyd University of Applied Sciences
Sittard, the Netherlands
martijn.zoet@zuyd.nl

Koen Smit
Digital Smart Services
HU University of Applied Sciences Utrecht
Utrecht, the Netherlands
koen.smit@hu.nl

Abstract— **This paper presents a cost/benefit analysis method for the normalization of business rules. To determine the economic benefit of business rules normalization three variables are addressed: 1) the number of anomalies a rule set endures, 2) the storage space a rule set requires and the 3) deterioration of rules in response time. The approach is evaluated by means of an experiment, based on mortgage data of an international bank. Results show that the method is useful for determining when to normalize business rule sets; the method enables business rules analysts to produce more cost-effective business rules architectures.**

Keywords-Business Rules; Decision Management; Normalization; Cost-Benefit Analysis

I. INTRODUCTION

Good decision making is a key denominator for a corporation's competitiveness [2]. Therefore, organizations are increasingly urged to make fast and accurate decisions. At the same time, decisions are becoming more and more complex affecting maintainability and transparency. Decisions can be formulated by means of business rules [22]. A business rule is defined by Morgan [13] as: "*a statement that defines or constrains some aspects of the business intending to assert business structure or to control the behavior of the business.*" To realize changes within an organization's decision-making process, an organization should be able to maintain the aforementioned asserts and it should be able to adapt its business rules efficiently and effectively to realize changes within its decision-making process. In order to realize this, information systems, such as expert systems, knowledge management systems, case based reasoning systems, fuzzy expert systems and business rules management systems have been built for and adopted by organizations [12].

Research on the management of business rules has been conducted since the mid-1960's [12]. Distinct research streams have emerged, focusing on the following three subjects: 1) subject transformation, 2) platform transformation, and 3) business rule model transformation [21]. Subject transformation research focuses on processes, methods and information systems used for mining and cleansing decision sources, such as regulations, organizational policies, laws, documents and databases. The second stream focuses on the use of information technology for the deployment, execution and monitoring of business rules. Important research topics are: 1) algorithms for faster and easier execution, 2) business rules architectures, and 3) business rules engines [1][6][15]. Business rule model transformation research focuses on verification, validation and improvement of existing business rules. To verify business rules, a formal grammar notation and/or a set of constructs is applied. A grammar notation describes how a business rule should be constructed or formulated. An example of a standardized business rules grammar is the Semantics of Business Vocabulary and Business Rules [16].

Despite the accumulation of literature, there is a surprisingly scarce amount of research that examines methods and processes to factor business rules [22]. Factoring entails the process of dividing business rules, and therefore decisions, in more comprehensible structural elements to increase maintainability and transparency. Research that has focused on this subject is "single language oriented" [21][22][23]. Since a relatively high number of business rules modelling languages exist within scientific and professional literature, a factoring procedure per language is not desired from the viewpoint of the authors. Furthermore, current research does not provide guidelines to financially quantify the value of factoring business rules. As far as the authors are aware, no method exists that is business rules modelling language-independent in combination with quantifying the financial benefits of factoring given business rules. An example is the work of [23] which solely focuses on achieving the third normal form while factoring business rules, without investigating whether this is financially optimal. Given the fact that organizations invest large amounts of money for implicitly managing business rules, a valid question is whether and when an explicit factoring procedure is economically beneficial. For example, a business rule set, which only changes or is executed twice a year might, from an economic perspective, is better off in an un-factored form. Taken previous statements into account, the following research question arose: "*How can business rules be factored such that economic beneficial manageability is realized?*" Following Van Thienen and Snoeck's [18] research on factoring decision tables and Zoet's [22] research on factoring business rules, we adopt relational theory to factor business rules.

The current study extends previous research by developing a factoring method that incorporates mainstream rule modeling languages and guidelines to determine the cost and revenue of (re-)factored business rules. We developed a factoring method and validated it by means of an experiment based on case study data at a large international bank. The results showed that our method is effective in determining the economic costs and benefits.

In section two, we provide a discussion on the theoretical foundations of factoring business rules in terms of relational theory, normalization and economic factors. This is followed by the construction of the method in section three. In section 4 we demonstrate the application of the method on mortgage decision making at a large international bank. We conclude this paper, in section five, with the study's core findings, contributions as well as its limitations.

II. Background and Related Work

There are few methods available to (re-)factor business rules [22]. Currently, two different methods are described: one by Van Thienen and Snoeck [18] and one by [22]. Van Thienen and Snoeck's [18] method has two underlying assumptions (1) business rules are specified in decision tables and (2) relational theory is the basis for normalizing business rules. Guidelines are proposed to factor decision tables, thereby improving maintainability. However, instead of formulating one common procedure they proposed multiple exceptions to the normal form. These exceptions have to be formulated, which is an implicit result of the foundation of their research namely the use of decision tables. The second method proposed by [22] also takes relation theory into account. Moreover, this method distinguishes itself by applying one common procedure, which can be used for several languages.

The definition of the term relational as used in this paper is adopted from the mathematical domain, more specifically from the relational algebra theory [4]. Relational algebra theory has received a lot of attention during the last four decades, since it is popularized by Codd [4] for database normalization. The basic idea of the relational algebra theory involves that a relationship (R) can exist of a given set of elements (Sn), visualized as follows: R = (S1, S2, ..., Sn) [4]. The elements (Sn) can be condition- or conclusion-facts. Most authors [4][9] represent element sets by applying two-dimensional arrays. In order to apply relational theory on business rules, one must be able to translate business rules to sets of relationships. Previous research has answered the question [22] whether current business rule modelling languages can be translated to unified views by applying relational algebra theory. Based on representational difference analysis, the authors show that the six most common business rules languages can be transformed to sets of relations. Representational difference analysis is a technique, which is used to identify differences and overlap between concepts or constructs in ontology's, languages and visual syntax [8] zur Muehlen and Indulska [20]. The six languages which were examined during this study are: If-Then business rules [17], Decision Tables [10] Van Thienen and Snoeck [18], Decision Trees [3], Score Cards [14], Event, Condition & Action Business Rules [5], and Event Condition Action Alternative Business Rules [7]. By translating business rules to relations between specific sets of elements, normalization is made possible. Normalization is the process of removing partial dependencies and transitive dependencies [4][9].

III. Method Construction

A detailed explanation of the business rules normalization procedure can be found in [22]. However, to ground our research, a summary of the normalization procedure is provided in sub-section A. Subsequently, in sub-section B, we described the cost reduction analysis method for business rules normalization.

A. *Business Rules Normalization Procedure*

The process for business rules normalization consists of three activities. The results of these activities are (1) the transformation of business rules to the proper relational structure, and (2) the removal of partial and (3) the removal of transitive dependencies. The latter is realized by applying the third normal form, while the second normal form deals with partial dependencies and the 1st normal form deals with achieving the proper structure for business rules.

The first normal form is realized by duplicating the original business rules equally often as the amount of conclusion-facts that exist. In other words, all of the duplicated rules exist of all condition- and conclusion-fields. The difference between the original and new tables is that only one of the original conclusion-fields is now still a conclusion-field while the others are condition-fields. In order for a relation to be in the second normal form, all condition-facts must be functionally dependent on a conclusion-fact and adhere to the first normal form. Condition-facts, which are not fully dependent on the conclusion-fact must be deleted or added to another relationship. The second normal form reveals whether condition-facts are included that actually do not contribute to a conclusion. To realize the third normal form in business rules, condition-facts that are not fully dependent on the conclusion-fact (but on another condition fact) should be removed and added to a new relation. The new relation contains the removed condition-facts, as well as the conclusion-fact to which they are related. A relationship is established between two sets of relations by means of a secondary decision. After applying the third normal form, all specified relations do not contain any repeating groups, partial dependencies and transitive dependencies anymore.

To visualize the normalization procedure a decision tree can be used [19]. A decision tree consists of two types of nodes: 1) normalization decision nodes (squares) and 2) end nodes (circles), for example see Fig. 1. A normalization decision node represents the decision to further normalize the relationship. From a normalization decision node, two types of branches can emerge: 1) a stop branch, and 2) a normalization branch. A stop branch emerges when further normalization is not needed, consequently leading to an end node. When further normalization is needed, two or more normalization branches emerge from the decision node. These branches lead to other decision nodes representing the newly normalized relationships.

End nodes do not have further identification information, whereas normalization decision nodes do. Each node starts with the capital letter R, which is an abbreviation for relationship. The digit before the decimal point shows the number of the relationship. In case two digits are included before the comma, it designates a relationship resulting from another relationship. Furthermore, the digit after the decimal point indicates in what normalization form the relationship resides. In our example (see Fig. 1), the node R1,2 means that relationship 1 is in the second normal form. Moreover, the nodes R11,3 and R12,3 are both in the third normal form and are a relationship resulting from R1,2.

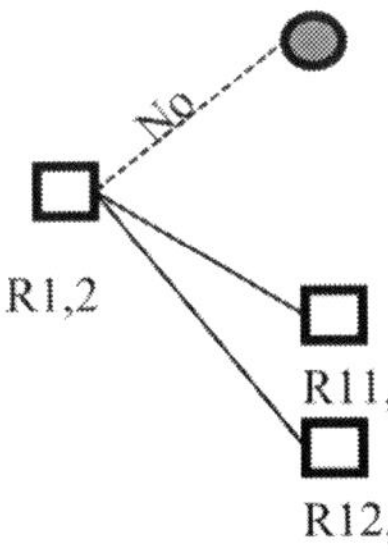

Figure 1. Decision Tree for Normalization

B. *Cost Reduction Analysis Method for Business Rules Normalization*

Currently, in most normalization procedures the decision to normalize is generally based on intuitive flair. It remains uncertain whether the normalization effort is economically beneficial. For example, from an economic perspective, a business rule set, which only changes twice a year may not be beneficial to normalize.

Lee [11] and Westland [19] have conducted research towards the cost reduction of *database* normalization, which is based on relational theory. Cost reductions realized by database normalization are 1) decreased machine time, and 2) decreased data-inconsistencies (avoiding loss of business). The three main drivers of cost reduction are a) reduced anomalies, b) reduced storage requirements, and c) deteriorated response time. Anomalies that occur to data are: update-anomalies, insert-anomalies and deletion-anomalies [4]. Previous research has shown that database normalization principles can be applied to business rule sets [22]. Taken previous statement into account, the following question arose: Can the cost reduction model from database normalization be adopted as well?

Before adopting and adapting the model for business rules normalization, first the fit between the database determinants and business rules determinants has to be investigated. First, both the relations of data and business rules need to be updated and deleted, and new data or business rules have to be inserted. Second, previous research [11] has shown that business rules normalization can also lead to fewer storage requirements, such as the case is with database normalization. Thirdly, deteriorated response time is an important issue since decision making in organizations is increasingly complex with for example predictive analytics. As such, we can adopt the formulas proposed by Lee [11]. However, before the formulas can be used, the variables need to be adapted towards business rules. The remainder of this section will discuss the formulas provided by Lee altered towards business rules.

The cost reduction realized by normalization is calculated in four phases 1) cost reduction due to reduced anomalies, 2) cost reduction due to reduced storage space, 3) cost increase due to increased join processing, and 4) comparing cost reduction due to reduced anomalies and cost reduction due to reduced storage space with the cost increase due to increased join processing.

Let ϕ be the cost reduction due to reduced anomalies, see also equation 1. We define ϕ as:

$$\phi = \sum_{M=1}^{Nu} \alpha_M^U \lambda_M^U \acute{\omega}_M^U + \sum_{M=1}^{Ni} \alpha_M^I \lambda_M^I \acute{\omega}_M^I + \sum_{M=1}^{Nd} \alpha_M^D \lambda_M^D \acute{\omega}_M^D$$

Equation 1. Cost reduction due to reduced anomalies

Where N_u, Ni, and Nd are the number of updates, number of inserts and number of deletions, respectively, λ_M^U, λ_M^I and λ_M^D denote the frequency of the m'th update, the m'th insertion and the m'th deletion. The average number of business rules affected by the update, insertion and deletion are denoted by $\acute{\omega}_M^U$, $\acute{\omega}_M^I$ and $\acute{\omega}_M^D$. Furthermore, α_M^U, α_M^I and α_M^D denote the cost for each insert, update and deletion.

Let ψ be the cost reduction due to reduced storage space, see also equation 2. We define ψ as:

$$\psi = B\acute{\omega} - B_x \acute{\omega}_x - B_y \acute{\omega}_y$$

Equation 2. Cost reduction due to reduced storage space

Where B represents the storage cost per business rule in the current normalized situation. B_x and B_y denote the storage cost per business rule in the normalized situation + 1. The number of business rules stored in the current normalization situation is depicted by $\acute{\omega}$, while the normalized situation + 1 is depicted by $\acute{\omega}_x$ and $\acute{\omega}_y$.

Let Ω be the cost increase due to increased join processing, see also equation 3. We define Ω as:

$$\Omega = \sum^{\emptyset}_{\substack{M=1 \\ x,y \in o^m}} \ddot{\Upsilon}_m \mu_m \acute{\omega}_x \acute{\omega}_y$$

Equation 3. Cost increase due to increased joint processing

Where $\emptyset$ is the number of joins required to determine the conclusion of a specific decision. $\ddot{\Upsilon}_m$ denotes the cost per execution per business rule for join M. Moreover, μ_m represents the frequency of join M. The time to realize the join is depicted by $\acute{\omega}_x$ and $\acute{\omega}_y$. The business rule sets (x and y) between which the join M is realized, is denoted by x, y, ϵ o^m. Let O be the cost reduction from normalization form R (R1,2) to normalization form R+1 (R11,3). We define O = ϕ + ψ $\geq$ Ω. O can be either positive or negative. If O is positive, then normalization should be applied.

IV. Experiment Setup

In our validation, we apply an experiment on case study data. This allows us to use data from an actual case while fully controlling the execution of the method and input variables. The method is applied to a mortgage decision of an Anonymous International Bank (AIB). Our choice to select this case study setting was based on two theoretical criteria. Firstly, the case had to provide a proper amount of business rules used to take a decision. The mortgage decision at AIB consisted of 665 facts (conditions and conclusions), and 1479 individual business rules. Secondly, the organization had to be willing to provide the financial details needed to perform the calculations. AIB agreed to this, however, with two demands. The first demand implied that their name and financial data were altered when it would be published. The second demand entailed that the applied business rule sets were not published. Since space limitations do not allow to walk through the entire mortgage decision and normalization procedure, both demands are met.

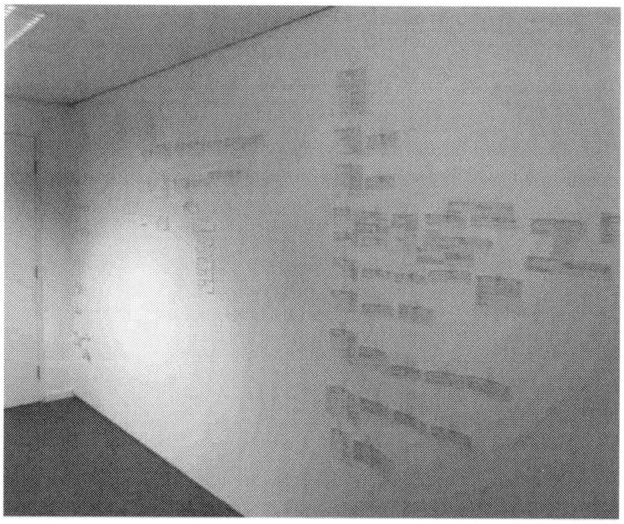

Figure 2. Photo impression 1 of normalized business rules

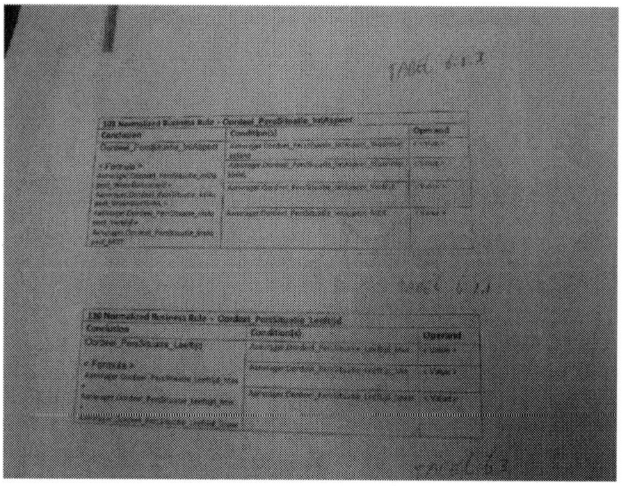

Figure 3. Photo impression 2 of normalized business rules

The evaluation, by means of conducting an experiment, was divided into three phases. Phase one was used to make the researchers familiar with the case parameters, by analyzing 133-pages with descriptions of decisions for completeness and accuracy. This phase resulted in the identification of multiple gaps. With the help of additional documentation and experts these gaps have been fixed. During the second phase, the business rules have been normalized according to our method. This normalization was done on paper after which the results were presented on a big wall (see Fig. 2 and Fig. 3). During the normalization, additional gaps were identified. These gaps have been marked with "post-its", see Fig. 2 and Fig. 3. Again, with the help of additional documentation and experts, these gaps have been filled.

V. APPLICATION OF THE METHOD

To ground our method, we explain the determination of the cost reduction from normalization form R to normalization form R+1 for the business rule set "personal situation of applicant" from the case described in the previous section. The business rule set exists of 10 facts, 1 conclusion fact and 8 condition facts; see left side of Fig. 4. The question that needs to be answered before normalizing this business rule set is: *"Does normalizing the business rule set from R to R+1 realize a cost reduction?"*

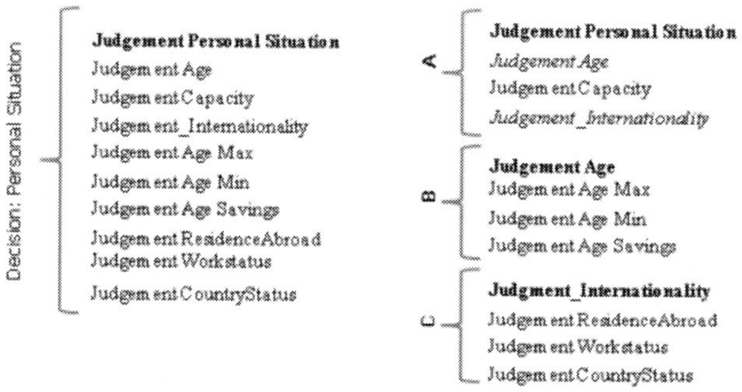

Figure 4. Decision tables to determine judgment personal situation

The decision personal situation is mainly affected by update and insert anomalies. For example, the facts "judgment age" and "judgment age savings" are updated regularly. Insert anomalies occur when new type of rules for age determination are inserted. The application of the method exist out of four phases 1) determine benefits in terms of reduced anomalies, 2) determine savings of storage requirements and 3) determine effect on response time, and 4) comparing cost reduction due to reduced anomalies and cost reduction due to reduced storage space with the cost increase due to increased join processing.

During phase one, three steps can be distinguished. *Step one:* determine the type of update, insert and deletion operations on a specific business rule set. In our case, "update judgment age" and "insert age determination rule". For each identified operation type, it should be determined if the operation is affected by anomalies. If anomalies do not occur, normalization is not needed at all. If anomalies do occur, the frequency of each operation type and the number of business rules that are affected should be determined, this corresponds to step *two*. In this specific case $\lambda_1^U = 7$ (/per 2 weeks), and $\lambda_2^U = 6$ (/ per 2 weeks). Additionally, the number of business rules affected by each update needs to be determined. In this specific case $\acute{\omega}_1^U = 2$ and $\acute{\omega}_2^U = 1.5$. During step *three*, the cost of an anomaly should be determined. In this case, the cost of a person that adjusts the specific business rules α_1^{U} = €35.00 per instance and α_2^{U} = €52.50 per instance, see also equation 4. So, the total benefit due to reduced number of anomalies is:

$$\phi = (35 * 7 * 2) + (52.5 * 6 * 1.5) = €962.50$$

Equation 4. Total benefit due to reduced anomalies

The first step of phase two is to determine the results of the transformation in terms of business rule sets. In this case, one business rule set (personal situation) is divided into three business rule sets namely 1) judgment personal situation, 2) judgment age, and 3) judgment internationality. The results of the normalization are shown in Fig. 3. For each business rule set, the number of business rules must also be determined, in this case, respectively, $\acute{\omega}$ = 20, $\acute{\omega}_x$= 2, $\acute{\omega}_y$= 3, $\acute{\omega}_z$= 6. During the second step, the cost per stored business rule must be determined. This needs to be determined for the current situation as well as for the post normalization situation. This information was retrieved from the information technology department, in this case, respectively, B = €4, B_X = €0,5, B_y = €0,5 and B_z = €0,75. Duplications are removed, thereby decreasing the number of individual business rules, see also equation 5. The total benefit due to reduced number of anomalies is:

$$\psi = 20 * 4 - 2 * 0.5 - 3 * 0.5 - 4 * 0.75 = €73.00$$

Equation 5. Total benefit due to reduced number of anomalies

To form a decision, two joins are required in the new situation, so $\emptyset$ =2. The cost for each join $\ddot{Y}_m$= 0.015. The execution frequency of the join is 4000 per two weeks (μ_m), see also equation 6. The additional cost due to additional join operations (Ω) is therefore:

$$\Omega = 0.015 * 4000 * (2 + 3 + 6) = €660.00$$

Equation 6. Total additional cost due to additional join operations

In conclusion, further normalization for the decision personal situation is recommended since (962.50 + 73.00) > €660.00. Assume a situation where λ_1^{U} = 7(/per 2 weeks), λ_2^{U}= 6 (/ per 2 weeks) are decreased to λ_1^{U} = 2(/per 2 weeks), λ_2^{U} = 2 (/ per 2 weeks). Applying these changes reduces ϕ from €962,50 to €446,25, which changes O from (962.50 + 73.00) > €660.00 to (446.25 + 73.00) < €660.00 in which case further normalization would not realize a cost reduction.

The above example has shown a situation in which normalization leads to cost reduction and therefore the normalization should occur. By changing two parameters, we showed that normalization would lead to a negative cost reduction therefore an increase in cost and normalization should not be performed.

VI. Experiment Validity

Internal validity threats, when conducting controlled experiments, can be classified into nine categories: 1) ambiguous temporal precedence, 2) selection, 3) history, 4) maturation, 5) regression, 6) attrition, 7) testing, 8) instrumentation, and 9) additive and interactive effect of threats to internal validity (Shadish et al., 2002). Ambiguous temporal precedence indicates a lack of clarity of variable occurrence, thereby influencing the cause and effect relation. In our research, temporal precedence occurs when decisions are transformed from source code to business rules management systems. The cost to realize an anomaly within the source code is higher compared to changing a business rule in a business rules management system. To reduce the temporal precedence, the source code was first transformed to be applicable for the business rules management systems, after which normalization took place. We can ensure that the learning effect was not present during our case. Given the fact that all four subjects who have participated in the experiment, already had executed the business normalization procedure before. Furthermore, the economical beneficially calculation itself was made explicit in Excel and required the respondents only to enter the variables. We cannot exclude learning during the transformation of the case information to the relational representation. Selection, history, maturation, attrition, instrumentation and additive and interactive effects of threats to internal validity are excluded due to the experiment setup.

Outcomes of an experiment can vary when subjects, tasks or the environment changes. External validity is concerned with the extension of variations on such changes (Shadish et al, 2002). Our results were obtained from one decision: a mortgage decision. Therefore, we cannot claim that our conclusions are generally applicable. However, the answer to the research question itself is not influenced by the fact that only one case has been analyzed. Our experiment has been applied outside the project life cycle of AIB. We do not consider this as a threat to environmental validity since the entire procedure can be repeated during normal project life cycles.

VII. Conclusion

Business rules are a key denominator for a corporation's competitiveness. Thereby, the management of such business rules is increasingly becoming more important. However, business rules are becoming more and more complex affecting maintainability and transparency. In order to properly structure business rules, normalization is applied. Normalization increases control over insertion, update and deletion anomalies affecting storage requirements and response time. Currently, the normalization procedure does not take the costs and benefits of normalization into account but is based on intuitive flair. Therefore, we defined the research question: How can business rules guiding decisions be factored such that economic beneficial manageability is realized?

We presented a cost/benefit formula that provides guidelines for normalizing business rules. To determine the normalization business case, three variables were addressed 1) the number of anomalies a business rule set endures, 2) the storage space a business rule set requires, and the 3) deterioration in response time. By means of an experiment based on case study data from an international bank, we have shown the applicability of the model. Results show the importance of properly normalized decisions and what role the cost and benefit analysis plays in this. On the one hand, modelers should attempt to properly factor business rules. To achieve this factoring, the three normalization forms can be applied. On the other hand, practitioners should take cost and benefits of the organization into account when applying such normalizations forms. Currently, the transformation of the business rules is performed manually. However, in future research we aim to develop an approach which applies an algorithm to re-write (transform) business rules for applying the method presented in this paper. Furthermore, future research should also focus on further validating the method presented in this paper using more cases, and ideally, cases from different industries in various sizes to improve its generalizability.

From a practical perspective, our study provides product engineers, business rules modelers and decision modelers with a method that can be used to normalize business rules based on an economic rationale. This rationale comprises the ideal fit between storage space utilization, anomaly management and execution costs. The method will enable organizations to guard, on the one hand, execution costs and, on the other hand, performance of business rules.

References

[1] D. Arnott, and G. Pervan, "A Critical Analysis of Decision Support Systems Research," Journal of Information Technology (20:2), pp. 67-87, 2005.

[2] M. W. Blenko, M. C. Mankins, P. Rogers, "The decision-driven organization," Harvard Business Review, 88(6), 54-62, 2010.

[3] J. Boyer, and H. Mili, "Agile Business Rules Development: Process, Architecture and Jrules Examples," Heidelberg: Springer, 2011.

[4] E. Codd, "A Relational Model of Data for Large Shared Data Banks," Communications of the ACM (13:6), pp. 377-387, 1970.

[5] U. Dayal, P. Buchmann, R. McCarthy, "Rules Are Objects Too: A Knowledge Model for an Active, Object-Oriented Database System," 2nd International Workshop on Object-Oriented Database Systems, K.R. Dittrich (ed.), Bad Münster am Stein-Ebernburg: Springer, pp. 129-143, 1988.

[6] I. Graham, "Business Rules Management and Service Oriented Architecture," New York: Wiley, 2006.

[7] T. Heimrich, and S. Günther, S, "Enhancing Eca Rules for Distributed Active Database Systems," NODe 2002 Web- and Database-Related Workshops, A. Chaudhri, M. Jeckle, E. Rahm and R. Unland (eds.), Erfurt: Springer, pp. 199-205, 2003.

[8] M. Hubank, and D. Schatz, "Identifying Differences in Mrna Expression by Representational Difference Analysis of Cdna," Nucleic Acids Research (22:5), pp. 5640-5648, 1994.

[9] W. Kent, "A Simple Guide to Five Normal Forms in Relational Database Theory," Communications of the ACM (6:2), pp. 120-125, 1983.

[10] R. Kohavi, "The Power of Decision Tables," 8th European Conference on Machine Learning Heraclion, N. Lavrac and S. Wrobel (eds.), Crete: Springer, pp. 174-189, 1995.

[11] H. Lee, "Justifying Database Normalization: A Cost/Benefit Model," Information Processing & Management (31:1), pp. 59-67, 1995.

[12] S. H. Liao, "Expert System Methodologies and Applications - a Decade Review from 1995 to 2004," Expert Systems with Applications (28:1), pp. 93-103, 2004.

[13] T. Morgan, "Business Rules and Information Systems: Aligning It with Business Goals," London: Addision-Wesley, 2002.

[14] D. Morrow, et al., "Timi Risk Score for St-Elevation Myocardial Infarction: A Convenient, Bedside, Clinical Score for Risk Assessment at Presentation," Circulation (10:2), pp. 2031-2037, 2000.

[15] M. L. Nelson, J. Peterson, R. L. Rariden, R. Sen, "Transitioning to a Business Rule Management Service Model: Case Studies from the Property and Casualty Insurance Industry," Information & Management (47:1), pp. 30-41, 2010.

[16] Object Management Group. "Semantics of Business Vocabulary and Business Rules (Sbvr), V1.0," Object Management Group, http://www.omg.org/spec/SBVR/1.0/PDF, retrieved Febrary, 2017.

[17] R. Rivest, "Learning Decision Lists," Machine Learning (2:3), pp. 229-246, 1987.

[18] J. Van Thienen, and M. Snoeck, "Knowledge Factoring Using Normalisation Theory," in: International Symposium on the Management of Industrial and Corporate Knowledge, IEEE (ed.). Compiegne: IEEE, 1993, 27-37.

[19] C. Westland, "Economic Incentives for Database Normalization," Information Processing & Management (28:5), pp. 647-662, 1992.

[20] M. zur Muehlen, and M. Indulska, "Modeling Languages for Business Processes and Business Rules: A Representational Analysis," Information Systems (35:4), pp. 379-390, 2010.

[21] M. M. Zoet, P. Ravesteyn, J. Versendaal "A Structured Analysis of Business Rules Representation Languages: Defining a Normalisation Form," Proceedings of ACIS, paper 20, 2011.

[22] M. M. Zoet, "Methods and Concepts for Business Rules Management," Utrecht: Hogeschool Utrecht, 2014.

[23] B. Von Halle, and L. Goldberg, "The Decision Model: A Business Logic Framework Linking Business and Technology," CRC Press, 2009.

Fundamental Constructs for Derivation Business Rules

Eline de Haan
Application Development
Dutch Tax and Customs Administration
Apeldoorn, the Netherlands
ey.de.haan@belastingdienst.nl

Martijn Zoet
Optimizing Knowledge-Intensive Business Processes
Zuyd University of Applied Sciences
Sittard, the Netherlands
martijn.zoet@zuyd.nl

Abstract—**Due to the creation of the new Decision Model Standard, derivation business rules play an even more crucial role in organizations' daily operations. To capture these business rules, organizations can choose between a multitude of commercially and scientifically available business rule languages. However, currently no set of criteria exists to evaluate these business rule languages and underlying tools with regard to expressiveness and preciseness. So, a need for a reference framework to simplify the selection process can be identified. During this research, a set of 15 fundamental constructs is identified, required to create precise and expressive business rules, which can be used as reference framework to perform an evaluation. The identified fundamental constructs have been validated in three different rounds using sequentially 37 patterns, 252 business rules, and six business rule management systems by applying Mill's Method, which indicated usefulness and completeness.**

Keywords-Business Rules; Fundamental Constructs; Business Rule Management; Business Rule Languages; Derivation Business Rules.

I. INTRODUCTION

More and more organizations capture their business logic in the form of business rules. A business rule is defined as: "*a statement that defines or constrains some aspect of the business, intending to assert business structure or to control the behavior of the business* [1]." In the last decade, these business rules have become an increasingly valuable asset for organizations. To specify and manage this asset, a multitude of business rule languages and systems is available. For instance: RuleSpeak, The Decision Model (TDM), the Simple Rule Markup Language (SRML), the Semantic Web Rules Language (SWRL), the Production Rule Representation (PRR), the Semantics of Business Vocabulary and Business Rules (SBVR), SRL, N3, and IRL [2].

The abundance of available systems and languages, and the fact that they differ to a large extent regarding their expressive power, causes two challenges. The first challenge organizations may encounter are difficulties in selecting an appropriate business rule management system or business rule language, since no set of criteria exists, which could be used as reference point for comparison. This can for instance lead to the selection of a language with a too extensive or too low level of expressive power. A second problem can occur when a language, tailored to a particular business rule management system, is selected. In case an organization transfers to a new or additional system, the business rules have to be re-specified to comply with the specification language of that specific system, which is highly inefficient, expensive and error prone.

Research has been initiated to compare the business rule languages, since various differences between the languages exist. Examples of such studies are [3] and [2]. Zoet et al. compared the representational capabilities of four different business rule languages [3], by mapping the fundamental elements of these languages onto the constructs of the Bunge-Wand-Weber (BWW) representation theory [4].

Previous studies focused on high-level elements (e.g., thing, property) of business rule languages. This view is applicable to analyze business rule languages at a global level, but not to evaluate the details of the syntax and semantics of the languages. Other previous studies focused on creating a business rule language that could cope with a whole range of logic. Examples of such languages are LISP and PROLOG [5]. However, much of the expressive power of these languages is not even applied in practice. This is caused by different factors, for instance: unusable for business users, but more importantly, most of this expressive power is not necessary to be able to specify derivation business rules.

The aim of this research is to evaluate business rule languages from a more detailed and practical view in order to tackle the outlined problems above. This research was conducted based on the following research question: *"How can derivation business rules be specified precisely and implementation independent?"*

This paper is organized as follows. Section II presents the literature review, which provides insight into different types of business rules and the specification thereof. Section III explains the applied research method to devise and validate the envisioned artifacts. The data collection and data analysis process are described respectively in Section IV and Section V. In Section VI, the results that derive from the identification and creation of artifacts are presented. Section VII provides the conclusions of the study including the contributions, limitations and future work.

II. Literature

In literature, a "business rule" is defined in a variety of ways, which is emphasized by a statement of Von Halle "*depending on whom you ask, business rules may encompass some or all relationship verbs, mathematical calculations, inference rules, step-by-step instructions, database constraints, business goals and policies, and business definitions* [6]." Furthermore, not one commonly accepted way to classify business rules exists. From literature, ten different classification schemes to classify business rules emerged, which each cover several business rule categories (types) [1][7][8][9][10][11][12]. Among the ten classification schemes, different names are used to refer to either similar or dissimilar business rule categories.

To delimit this research, the focus will lie on one specific type of business rules namely **derivation business rules**. A derivation business rule can be defined as: "*an expression that evaluates facts, by means of a calculation or classification, leading to a new fact (i.e., conclusion) [1][13].*" To position the type of business rule on which this research focuses, derivation business rules, this type is compared to the categories included in the ten found classification schemes. This comparison showed that derivation business rules correspond to the following categories of the found classification schemes: 1) Inference rules, 2) Computation rules, 3) Derivation rules, 4) Classification rules, 5) Decision rules, 6) Calculation rules, and 7) Rounding rules [1][7][8][11][12][14].

Besides the fact that different business rule definitions and categories exist, also many different business rule notation forms are available to specify derivation business rules. At the highest abstraction level, two main formalism types can be identified: implementation dependent and implementation independent languages. The first type is defined as "*an implementation dependent language is a language that complies to a specific software formalism, has a delimited predefined expressiveness, and is tailored to be interpreted by a particular information system* [15]." Examples of implementation dependent languages are LISP and Haskell, but also the languages used by specific business rule (management) systems, such as Corticon or Be Informed. When organizations use such an implementation dependent language and switch to a new business rule management system, the business rules must be re-specified in order for this system to process them, which is highly inefficient, expensive and error prone. In contrast, an implementation independent language is considered as: "*a language that complies with a certain level of naturalness but has a delimited predefined expressiveness and is not tailored to be applicable for a specific automated information system* [15]." So, this second formalism could by applied in multiple environments addressing the disadvantages of a dependent language but is generally not **precise** enough to be directly executable by an automated information system.

A solution for this problem can be found by investigating which fundamental constructs (i.e., building blocks of a language) are necessary to specify a precise derivation business rule. Similar studies are performed in different research fields concerning fundamental constructs. For example, Moody created a checklist comprising a defined set of criteria to determine if a language can be easily understood by people [27]. Furthermore, Van der Aalst created a list of patterns to check if business process management systems could handle different types of process elements [28]. Like in the previous studies, our goal is not to create a new language. However, the focus will lie on the identification of the minimal set of constructs a language needs to contain to be able to precisely specify business rules found in practice. When this minimal set of fundamental constructs is used as reference point to select a language, it should be made clear that not all these constructs have to be included in the language. In some cases, these constructs are already available as property in the business rule (management) system. For example, in tools like Be Informed and Berkely Bridge the relationship between constructs cannot be expressed by means of the language but only by the use of a system property.

III. Research Method

The purpose of this research is to identify the fundamental constructs that characterize a precise and transformable derivation business rule. The premise of this research is that the identified set of fundamental constructs is good enough when most common business rules in practice can be captured. To accomplish this goal, a research approach is needed that can identify 1) the fundamental constructs applied in business rules and 2) the similarities and dissimilarities between fundamental constructs applied in business rules.

Both requirements can be met by applying grounded theory. The purpose of grounded theory is to "*explain with the fewest possible concepts, and with the greatest possible scope, as much variation as possible in the behavior and problem under study [16].*" Grounded theory identifies differences and similarities by applying eighteen coding families. However, this does not provide a structured comparison of the identified situational factors across cases. Therefore, an additional technique is needed to compare the differences between a variety of business rules. A technique specifically engineered to inspect cases for similarities and differences is ordinal comparison based on Mill's method of agreement and difference [17]. Mill's methods are used to draw conclusions about causal relationships by analyzing the data (i.e., effects) and find common denominators (i.e., causes) [18]. With regard to this research, the common denominators correspond to the required fundamental constructs found in each case to be able to specify precise derivation business rules.

IV. Data Collection

Three rounds of data collection were performed. The first data set comprised existing business rule patterns, these were collected in order to identify the first set of fundamental constructs. For the second data set, existing business rules were gathered to analyze if the identified fundamental constructs could cover the business rules or additional constructs were needed. For the third data set, business rules were collected, which were implemented in a specific business rule management system, to examine the applicability of the identified fundamental constructs in an implementation dependent environment.

To select the data sets, one overall practical selection criterion was applied namely *site/document access* to be able to use the data for this research. In contrast, the applied theoretical selection criteria differed per data set. For the first data set, one theoretical criterion was taken into account, which meant that solely business rule patterns focused on specifying derivation business rules were included. Based on this criterion, 37 patterns from the following five current existing business rule pattern catalogues were selected: [8][11][12][14][19]. Table I shows the amount of collected patterns per catalogue.

TABLE I. AMOUNT OF PATTERN COLLECTED PER CATALOGUE.

Pattern Catalogue	Amount of Patterns
Morgan	2
RuleSpeak	12
Wan Kadir & Loucopoulos	2
Von Halle	2
RegelSpraak	19
TOTAL	37

For the second data set, one theoretical selection criterion was applied: only instantiations of derivation business rules were eligible. By adhering to this criterion, 252 derivation business rules were randomly selected from the following eleven different business rule cases originating from both literature and practice: [8][11][12][14][19][20][21][22][23][24][25]. This sampling strategy is followed in order to cover a wide range of domains where business rules are utilized. Table II lists the amount of selected business rules per case.

With regard to the third data set, two theoretical criteria were applied. The first theoretical criterion to select the business rule management systems implied that the documentation of each system covered the implementation of the same business rule set (i.e., use case). The second theoretical selection criterion corresponded to the fact that the business rule set had to comprise derivation business rules. As result, implementation documentation including 69 derivation business rules was collected of the following six business rule management systems: 1) Blueriq, 2) Corticon, 3) IBM ODM, 4) Sapiens, 5) OpenRules, and 6) OpenL Tablets.

TABLE II. AMOUNT OF BUSINESS RULES COLLECTED PER CASE.

Business Rule Case	Amount of Business Rules
Morgan	4
RuleSpeak	11
Wan Kadir & Loucopoulos	4
Von Halle	9
RegelSpraak	19
WereWolf	16
Diabetic Patient Monitoring	6
Patient Therapy	12
Tax Return	32
Au pair	1
UServ Product Derby	138
TOTAL	252

V. Data Analysis

The data analysis comprised three different validation rounds. For each validation round, the same coding procedure and scheme were applied. The coding procedure was established together with a second researcher and based on the Joint Method of Agreement and Difference of [18]. Due to space limitations, only an excerpt of the coding scheme is shown in Figure 1 and Figure 2 including two example business rules from the second validation round.

Derivation Business Rule															
Conclusion Part															
	Quantifier	Subject	Relation	Modal Claim Type	Expression										
					Classification					Ground					
					Propositional Operator	Value	Quantifier	Subject	Relation	Mathematical Operator	Mathematical Function	Value	Quantifier	Subject	Relation
1	the	car	's	-	is	high	-	-	-	-	-	-	-	-	-
		potential theft rating													
2	The	total amount	of	-	-	-	-	-	-	is computed as	the sum of	-	the	bill item amount	-
	a	bill													

Figure 1. Example mapping of Business Rules on Conclusion Part.

Derivation Business Rule																
Condition Part																
	Construct	Quantifier	Subject	Relation	Connective	Expression										
						Classification					Ground					
						Propositional Operator	Value	Quantifier	Subject	Relation	Mathematical Operator	Mathematical Function	Value	Quantifier	Subject	Relation
1	if	the	car	-	-	is	convertible	-	-	-	-	-	-	-	-	-
2	-	-	-	-	-	-	-	-	-	-	-	-	-	-	-	-

Figure 2. Example mapping of Business Rules on Condition Part.

The coding scheme is split up for readability reasons into two separate tables, where the orange and green cells contain the fundamental constructs and the white cells the data item parts (i.e., business rule parts). The first example business rule (see row no. 1 in Fig. 1 and Fig. 2) corresponds to the coding of the following derivation business rule of the UServ Product Derby case: *"The car's potential theft rating is high if the car is convertible."* To code this business rule, the conclusion and condition part were identified first where "the car's potential theft rating is high" corresponds to the conclusion part (see Figure 1) and "if the car is convertible" to the condition part (see Figure 2). Subsequently, the conclusion and condition part were disassembled in smaller parts, which were matched onto the fundamental constructs of the coding scheme. For example, the fundamental construct *Quantifier* is two times included as "the" and three instantiations of the fundamental construct *Subject* are identified namely "car", "potential theft rating" and "car".

Although the same coding procedure and scheme were applied for every validation round, some differences can be appointed between the three rounds with regard to the process. During the first round, one researcher coded the 37 collected business rule patterns. In case the researcher was not certain about the coding of particular parts, a second researcher was consulted and the coding process was continued. Subsequently, this second researcher coded a few randomly selected business rule patterns, which were compared with the coded variant of the first researcher. Any discrepancies were discussed until agreement was reached. For the second round, three researcher were involved namely the two researcher of the first round and one additional researcher. This additional researcher acted as reliability coder since the outcome of the coding could be influenced by the mindset and convention of the researcher after the first round. Involving a reliability coder could reduce this effect and could enhance the reliability of the results [26]. So, the 252 selected business rules were coded by both the first researcher and the reliability coder applying the same coding procedure. Besides the use of this coding procedure, the first researcher coded and explained a few example business rules to the reliability coder in advance to ensure that the coding was performed in exactly the same way. After both mappings were conducted, the results were compared and the differences were discussed among all three researchers until agreement was reached again. Prior to the third validation round, a few data items were coded together by the two researchers of the first round. Then, the entire coding procedure of the implemented version of business rules from the implementation documentation of the six selected business rule management systems was completed by the first researcher. Same as applied for the first round, the second researcher was consulted when obscurities emerged. Finally, the second researcher randomly validated a few coded data items. Any anomalies were discussed until agreement was reached, after which the third coding round was finalized.

VI. Results

In this section, the 15 fundamental constructs that are identified to specify a precise and implementation independent derivation business rule are described, which are: conclusion part, condition part, subject, quantifier, relation, expression, classification, value, propositional operator, ground, mathematical operator, mathematical function, modal claim type, construct and connective.

A derivation business rule is composed of two fundamental constructs on the highest abstraction level: the conclusion part and condition part. In the example business rule of Figure 3, the conclusion part is denoted by an orange border and the condition part by a green border. In literature, the conclusion part is also referred to as 'conclusion assertion' or 'then-part', and the condition part as 'if-part' or 'when-part' [3][13]. The conclusion part and condition part are further specified with specific underlying fundamental constructs, which are described in the remainder of this section.

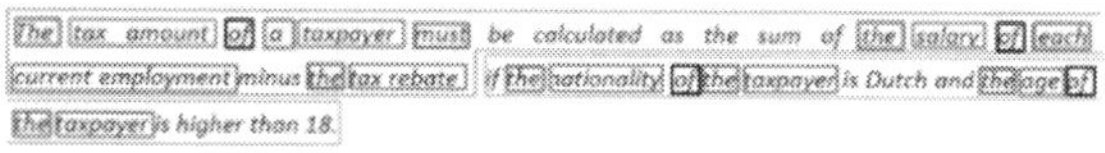

Figure 3. Example business rule indicating the fundamental constructs.

A. Subject

The *subject* is the most fundamental part of a business rule. A *subject* is "*a noun, a thing with an agreed-upon definition, a recognizable business entity* [13][14]." It refers to the business entity on which a conclusion is drawn, as well as the condition(s) that should be applied to reach this conclusion. In the example business rule, subjects are denoted by a blue border, for example: tax amount, taxpayer, and salary (see Fig. 3). In the business rule pattern catalogues and literature, several different names are found to refer to a *subject* like: term, subject, result, value, subj, property of a concept, entity, and attribute [8][11][14].

B. Quantifier

The subject indicates which business entity is applied, the *quantifier* indicates how many or which specific instantiation of the business entity must be applied. This can for example be a specific subject (i.e., **the** subject), one subject (e.g., **a/an** subject) or more subjects (e.g., **each/every** subject). In the example business rule, each quantifier is denoted by a red border (see Fig. 3). In the pattern catalogue of Morgan, this fundamental construct is called a *determiner* [14], and in the business rule language SBVR a *keyword* [10].

C. Relation

In the majority of studied business rules, multiple subjects were present. See for example the business rule in Fig. 3, which includes the subjects "tax amount" and "tax payer". The purpose of this business rule is to conclude something about the combination of both, namely the "tax amount of the tax payer." The question that arises is if this combination must be seen as one subject or as two individual subjects. In practice, both solutions to this problem can be recognized. However, the choice to include subject as a single fundamental construct in the identified set to refer to both "concepts (i.e., entities)" and "properties of concepts (i.e., attributes)", can have a disadvantage. Although it keeps the amount of fundamental constructs limited, it can also make the business rule ambiguous. Therefore, some practitioners choose to add an additional fundamental construct, which addresses this disadvantage. This fundamental construct specifies the relation between subjects. By means of this relation, the different granularity levels between subjects can be made clear again. Since it is necessary to be able to precisely specify the relation between subjects in a business rule, ensuring an unambiguous and precise business rule, the fundamental construct *relation* is added. This relation is shown by means of a black border in Fig. 3.

D. Expression

Taking the definition of a derivation business rule into account , "*an expression that evaluates facts, by means of a calculation or classification, leading to a new fact (i.e., conclusion)* [1][13]", both the calculation and classification fundamental construct are seen as a specific type of *expression*. Considering this definition, two statements can be made: 1) facts in a derivation business rule are evaluated by means of a calculation or classification, and 2) a new fact (i.e., conclusion) of a derivation business rule is either determined by a *calculation* or a *classification*. Both the *calculation* and the *classification* are seen as a separate fundamental construct of a derivation business rule, where the calculation is called a *ground*. The fundamental construct is called a *ground* since it has several underlying fundamental constructs, therefore names like computation or calculation are considered as too narrow.

E. Classification

A specific type of expression is the *classification*. On the one hand, in the conclusion part a classification can equate a subject with another subject or a value. For example: "*Food Intake Risk Points of the patient must be equated to 2.*" In this example, the subject Food Intake Risk Points is equated to the value 2. On the other hand, in the condition part a classification can check the consistency between a subject and another subject or a value. For example: "*If Solid Intake of the patient is equal to 5 days.*" In this case, the subject Solid Intake is compared to the value 5.

F. Propositional Operator

To be able to make the difference between the two classification options (i.e., equate with or check the consistency) clear, a fundamental construct is included. This fundamental construct is called a *propositional operator*, which is underlined in the example business rules above.

G. Value

A fundamental construct that emerged from the coding exercise is *value*. Von Halle and Goldberg refer to a value by the word 'fact' or 'fact value' [13]. The fundamental construct *value* is added to distinguish between constants and variables. Where value is a constant and subjects are used to denote variables.

H. Ground

The second type of expression is the *ground*. On the one hand, in the conclusion part a *ground* can equate a subject with a basic ground. For example: "*Malnutrition Risk Points of the patient must be computed as Weight Loss Risk Points of the patient + Body Mass Index Risk Points of the patient.*" On the other hand, in the condition part a ground can compare a subject with another subject, a value, or a basic ground. For example: "*IF Weight Loss of the patient is less than 5%.*"

I. Mathematical Operator and Mathematical Function

To be able to make the difference between the two ground options (i.e., equate with and compare with), a fundamental construct is included. This fundamental construct is called a mathematical operator, which is underlined in the business rules above. In addition to *mathematical operators*, also more sophisticated calculations have to be made. For example: sum, median or cosines. These are called mathematical functions. Since business rule management systems make a difference between the two, both fundamental constructs are included.

J. Modal Claim Type

The fundamental construct *modal claim type* is only applicable for the conclusion part and not for the condition part. This fundamental construct determines how the derivation business rule is imposed. In other words, this fundamental construct defines the modality of the business rule. Examples of these modality options, which occurred during the coding exercise, are: "must" to formulate an obligation or "may" to formulate a permission. In the example business rule of Fig. 3, the modality is denoted by a purple border. By explicitly specifying the modality of a business rule, the intention of the business rule becomes clearer for humans. However, excluding the modality will not change the logic of the business rule. When 'must' is excluded from the example business rule (see Fig. 3), only the representation will change.

K. Construct

The fundamental construct called *construct* is used to indicate a condition part of the business rule, which is repeatedly found in business rule catalogues or languages. Most pattern catalogues only include specific instantiations for this fundamental construct and no overall name is given. For instance, Morgan includes the instantiations 'if or unless' to indicate the condition part [14]. Solely the RuleSpeak pattern catalogue of Hoppenbrouwers provides an overall name for such instantiations namely keywords, which covers the following three: if, when and only if [19]. In computer science, or more specifically with regard to programming languages, the above provided instantiations are commonly referred to as constructs.

L. Connective

In some business rules more than one condition is included, for example: "*IF Age of the patient is equal to 18 AND Liquid Intake of the patient is more than 1 day.*" In these cases, the connection between these conditions has to be made clear. Does only one condition has to be met, or a few of them, or maximal one. To indicate the relation between the conditions, the fundamental construct *connective* is added.

VII. Discussion and Conclusion

This research investigated the fundamental constructs of derivation business rules with the purpose of developing a reference framework to evaluate existing business rule languages and business rule management systems. To accomplish this goal, a grounded theory study was executed to derive the minimal set of fundamental constructs needed to define a precise and implementation independent business rule that can be transformed (automatically) to an implementation dependent business rule. The analysis revealed 15 fundamental constructs that are required to do so. Although the three performed validation rounds and the amount of used input data for each round are considered as sufficient (i.e., 37 patterns, 252 business rules, and 6 systems), the size of each data set could be increased for further research to enhance the generalization of the results even further. We believe that this work represents a further step in research on business rule management. Future research will focus on the formulation of patterns including the fundamental constructs. The patterns can be applied to consistently and unambiguously formulate business rules and evaluate the expressiveness of business rule management systems.

References

[1] D. Hay, and K. Healy, *Defining Business Rules: What are they really?* (Revision 1.3). [Online]. Available from http://www.businessrulesgroup.org/first_paper/BRG-whatisBR_3ed.pdf: the Business Rules Group 2016-05-15

[2] M. zur Muehlen, and M. Indulska, "Modeling Languages for Business Processes and Business Rules: A Representational Analysis," Information Systems (35:4), pp. 379-390, 2010.

[3] M. Zoet, P. Ravesteyn, and J. Versendaal, "A Structured Analysis of Business Rules Representation Languages: Defining a Normalization Form." Proc. of the Twentieth Australasian Conference on Information Systems (ACIS 2013), Sydney, pp. 1-10.

[4] Y. Wand, and R. Weber, "On the ontological expressiveness of information systems analysis and design grammars," Information Systems Journal (3:4), pp. 217-237, 1993.

[5] D. Warren, L. Pereira, and F. Pereira, "Prolog-the language and its implementation compared with Lisp." ACM SIGART Bulletin (12:64), pp. 109-115, 1977.

[6] B. Von Halle, "Back to Business Rule Basics." Database Programming & Design, pp. 15-18, 1994.

[7] J. Boyer, and H. Mili, Agile Business Rules Development: Process, Architecture and JRules Examples. Heidelberg: Springer, 2011.

[8] B. Von Halle, Business Rules Applied: Building Better Systems Using the Business Rules Approach. New York: Wiley, 2001.

[9] F. Caron, J. Vanthienen, and B. Baesens, "Comprehensive Rule-Based Compliance Checking and Risk Management with Process Mining." Decision Support Systems (54:3), pp. 1357-1369, 2013.

[10] Object Management Group. *Semantics of Business Vocabulary and Business Rules (SBVR) (v1.2)*. [Online]. Available from: http://www.omg.org/spec/SBVR/1.2/ 2016-04-04.

[11] W. Wan-Kadir, and P. Loucopoulos, "Relating Evolving Business Rules to Software Design." Journal of Systems Architecture (50:7), pp. 367-382, 2004.

[12] G. Sangers-van Cappellen, "RegelSpraak (v3.2)." Internal publication of The Dutch Taxation Office, Belastingdienst, 2014.

[13] B. Von Halle and L. Goldberg, The Decision Model: A Business Logic Framework Linking Business and Technology. London: CRC Press, 2009.

[14] T. Morgan, "Business Rules and Information Systems: Aligning It with Business Goals," London: Addision-Wesley, 2002.

[15] M. Zoet, "Methods and Concepts for Business Rules Management," Utrecht: Hogeschool Utrecht, 2014.

[16] B. Glaser, "Theoretical Sensitivity: Advances in the Methodology of Grounded Theory," Mill Valley, CA: Sociology Press, 1978.

[17] J. Mahoney, "Nominal, Ordinal, and Narrative Appraisal in Macrocausal Analysis." American Journal of Sociology (104:4), p.p. 1154-1196, 1999.

[18] J. Mill, A system of Logic, London: Longmans Green, 1906.

[19] S. Hoppenbrouwers, "RuleSpeak grammar." Internal Publication of the Radboud University, Radboud University Nijmegen, 2011.

[20] B. Bouvier. *Decision Model: Determine the Risk of Meeting a Werewolf.* [Online]. Available from: https://dmcommunity.wordpress.com/ 2014-09-09

[21] Business Rules Forum. *Version 2 UServ Product Derby Case Study* [Online]. Available from: http://ai.ia.agh.edu.pl/wiki/_media/hekate:2005_product_derby.pdf 2015-01-04

[22] M. Parish. *Rule Modeling Case Study Generic Diabetic Monitoring (v1.0)*. [Online]. Available from: https://dmcommunity.wordpress.com/case-studies/#DiabeticPatientMonitoring 2015-01-04

[23] J. Feldman. *Preparing a Tax Return (Release 6.1)*. [Online]. Available from: http://openrules.cm/pdf/Tutorial.Dialog1040EZ.pdf: OpenRules 2015-12-12

[24] J. Feldman. *Determine Patient Therapy (Release 6.3.0)*. [Online]. Available from: http://openrules.com/pdf/Tutorial.DecisionPatientTherapy.pdf : OpenRules 2015-12-12

[25] P. Klaasen, "Internal Rules to Determine proffesion of Au Pair" Internal publication of Anonymous Dutch government organization, 2014.

[26] N. Mays, and C. Pope, "Qualitative Research: Rigour and Qualitative Research." BMJ (311:6997), pp. 109-112, 1995.

[27] D. Moody, *"The "physics" of notations: toward a scientific basis for constructing visual notations in software engineering. IEEE Transactions on Software Engineering,"* (35:6), pp. 756-779, 2009.

[28] W. Van der Aalst, A. Ter Hofstede, B. Kiepuszewski, B. and P. Barros. Workflow Patterns. "Distributed and parallel databases" (14:1), pp. 5-51, 2013.

Predicting Corporate Bond Prices in Japan Using a Support Vector Machine

Hiroaki Jotaki
Department of Computational Intelligence and Systems Science, Interdisciplinary Graduate School of Science and Engineering
Tokyo Institute of Technology
Kanagawa, Japan
e-mail: Hiro.jotaki@gmail.com

Yasuo Yamashita
Investment Research Department
Sumitomo Mitsui Trust Bank
Tokyo, Japan
e-mail: Yamashita_Yasuo@smtb.jp

Hiroshi Takahashi
Graduate School of Business Administration
Keio University
Kanagawa, Japan
e-mail: htaka@kbs.keio.ac.jp

Abstract—**Predictability of returns is one of the most important concerns in bond investment. In this study, we analyze the predictability of corporate bond prices after company announcements of financial results using a support vector machine (SVM). This paper will discuss (1) the highest hit ratio found when predicting the movement of corporate bond prices using the four variables of current net earnings, management earnings forecasts, ratings, and a leading composite index, and (2) the highest hit ratio found while using a Gaussian kernel function with a parameter of 0.6 and a slack coefficient of 1.0. In addition to offering captivating insights from the results of this study regarding the mechanism by which financial reports impact prices in the bond market, our results also deepen our understanding of excess returns in asset management.**

Keywords-Corporate Bonds; Prediction; SVM.

I. INTRODUCTION

In the management of corporate bonds, ensuring stable generation of excess profits, identifying sources of excess returns, and predicting credit risk are all critical concerns [1][2][3][4][5].

Research on sources of excess profits is closely related to discussions of market efficiency, and numerous studies focusing primarily on stocks, have been conducted on this topic [6][7]. Among these, the relationship between company financial reports and the stock market is one of the areas where research is most extensive [8][9][10]. Several studies have been conducted on the impact of financial statements on the stock market, but there are few studies that focus on the bond market. Reference [3] focuses on information disclosed in company financial reports in Japan and conducts an event study analysis using the cumulative excess return (CER) to analyze the impact of disclosure information on corporate bond prices. As a result, it found that corporate bond prices tend to exhibit (1) no change in CER if current net earnings are higher than the previous term, while CER tends to become negative if current net earnings are less than the previous term, and (2) CER becomes increasingly negative when current net earnings decrease, management earnings forecasts for the next term are less optimistic, and bond ratings are low. This shows that current net earnings impact bond prices more than management earnings forecasts.

Research regarding price predictability is also a critical stream, and numerous studies have been conducted mainly focusing on stocks. Traditional prediction methods include regression models and auto regression models, but more recently, studies using learning models have also become popular. References [11][12] have predicted stock prices using support vector machines (SVM) and have reported that the accuracy of such predictions is higher compared with traditional models. However, these studies were conducted outside of the Japanese market, and studies regarding the predictability of corporate bond prices in Japan are particularly rare.

To address this gap, this study analyzes the predictability of Japanese corporate bond prices following announcements of financial results using a SVM.

The structure of the rest of this paper is as follows. The analytical methods used are explained in Section II, and the study results are discussed in Section III. A summary of our study is presented in Section IV.

II. ANALYTICAL METHOD

After first characterizing the samples used in the analysis and the corporate bond CER, we describe the four factors used as explanatory variables: current net earnings, management earnings forecasts, the index of business conditions, and ratings.

A. *Sample*

The sample data used in this study are comprised of reported corporate financial results disclosed between 2002 and 2010. The data used comes from 1,441 companies that satisfied the following five conditions: (1) from company annual reports that had at least two reporting periods between 2002 and 2010, (2) from companies that disclose current earnings and earnings forecasts per share on a consolidated basis (or nonconsolidated basis if unavailable), (3) from companies whose rate of change in the number of shares in comparison to the previous fiscal year was 20% or lower, (4) from the companies which issued one or more bonds with one year or more remaining maturity, and 5) from companies that have been rated (R&I standard).

TABLE I. NO. OF SAMPLE

		Current net earnings		
		Increased	Decreased	Total
Net earnings forecast	Increased	583	474	1057
	Decreased	267	117	384
Total		850	591	1441

B. Corporate bond CERs

In this section, we define the annual reporting date as daily 0 (t=0) and then analyze the return on bond j issued by company i. The belief is that information around financial results affects the corporate bond spread, representing corporate credit risk.

Therefore, we focus on bond returns as a function of changes in corporate bond spreads. Corporate bond spreads are calculated based on the difference between the corporate bond yield and the government bond yield whose maturity is the same as the corporate bond and can be converted into returns by multiplying the change in the spread by the price sensitivity (Mdur) against the yield. However, in order to focus on changes in the corporate bond spread resulting from information disclosed by individual companies, it is necessary to calculate the return on bonds (hereafter "excess return") by deducting the effect of changes in the overall market spread. References [13][14] defined excess return as the difference between the total return on corporate bonds and the total return on bond indices with the same rating and maturity as the corporate bonds. Because Japanese bond indices are separated by rating and maturity and therefore have different spreads, in this study, we decided to determine excess returns based on corporate bond spreads with reference to the method described by [13][14].

Equation (1) is used to calculate excess returns on corporate bonds. The excess return on corporate bond j issued by company i is obtained by subtracting the index spread total return (ISR) from the spread total return (SR) of issuer i.

$$er(i, j, t) = SR(i, j, t) - ISR(i, j, t). \quad (1)$$

Equation (2) is used to calculate the SR of corporate bonds used in (1) above. The first variable in (2) represents the capital return coming from the spread, and the second variable represents the income return from the spread. Mdur represents the modified duration.

$$SR(i,j,t) = dSR \times Mdur + Spd \times days/365. \quad (2)$$

Equation (3) is used to calculate the ISR of the index used in (1). In this analysis, NOMURA-BPI data are used as index data. The R&I standard rating (AA, A, BBB, BB), the maturity (short term(less than 1-3 years), middle term (>3, <7 years), or long term (>7 years)) can be obtained as index attribute information by spread. We calculated the returns for each category based on information from these 12 types of spreads.

$$ISR = dSpd \times Mdur + Spd \times days/365. \quad (3)$$

Additionally, if company i is issuing J bonds, the excess return on individual bond j issued by the same company is weighted based on market value of bond j at time t, and the excess return on the bond issued by company i is then calculated. W represents the weighted market value of the bond j.

$$Er(i, t) = \Sigma w(i, j, t) \times er(i, j, t). \quad (4)$$

The average excess return at time t (at time of reporting: t = 0) is as follows.

$$ER(t) = \Sigma\, Er(i, t) \;/\; N. \quad (5)$$

CER is defined as the cumulative return of ER(t) obtained in this manner on a daily basis.

C. Corporate bond CERs on a yearly basis

During the sample period 2002 to 2010, the economic situation varied depending on the year. Thus, there is a possibility that reactions in the corporate bond market differ depending on economic conditions. For example, based on the economic cycle announced by the Cabinet Office in Japan, it is possible to divide the cycle into two segments: an expansion phase and a recession phase. Based on this schema, 2002 was the bottom of the recession phase and the economy exhibited growth until 2008. However, after the Lehman shock that occurred in 2008, the economy went into a decline. The recession phase continued until 2009, and the economy then entered an expansion phase in 2010.

In this section, we will analyze the CER trend for making predictions of corporate bond CER. Specifically, we divide CERs by fiscal year, and further divide these based on movement in current net earnings (increase, decrease) and management earnings forecasts (increase, decrease). We assume here that investments are made the day following the announcement of financial results, and the cumulative excess return is CER (+1, +30).

We look at these results in the context of management next term earnings forecasts based on an increase in current net earnings. During the economic expansion phase, CERs tend to be positive regardless of the increase or decrease in the next term earnings forecast, but the CER may be negative during a recession phase. Next, we looked at the results in the context of management next term earnings forecasts based on a decrease in current net earnings. When compared on an annual basis, the tendency is that no change in CER is observed, or the CER may be negative. Particularly in 2002 and 2009, during the economic recession, we can see that the CER is strongly negative in the case when the management earnings forecast decreased. This indicates that corporate bond prices may be affected by economic conditions as well as current net earnings and earnings forecasts.

TABLE II. CORPORATE BOND CERS ON A YEARLY BASIS

CER(+1,+30)

	current net earnings	net earnings forecast	2002	2003	2004	2005	2006	2007	2008	2009	2010
(a)	+	+	-0.383%	0.167%	0.033%	0.042%	-0.016%	0.008%	-0.044%	-0.950%	0.211%
			(-3.9)	(2.7)	(1.9)	(4.5)	(-0.9)	(0.4)	(-0.3)	(-4.1)	(3.5)
		N	65	89	102	87	65	63	39	14	59
(b)	〃	—	-0.186%	0.075%	0.029%	0.043%	0.088%	-0.041%	-0.179%	-0.255%	0.287%
			(-2.9)	(2.1)	(1.3)	(2.8)	(1.0)	(-1.8)	(-0.5)	(-0.7)	(1.8)
		N	19	36	34	35	40	36	40	13	14
(c)	—	+	-0.248%	0.092%	0.008%	0.020%	-0.029%	-0.078%	-0.005%	-0.338%	0.177%
			(-5.2)	(1.8)	(0.7)	(1.8)	(-1.2)	(-1.2)	(-0.1)	(-1.5)	(2.8)
		N	96	51	42	42	49	35	49	71	39
(d)	〃	—	-0.379%	0.100%	0.048%	-0.029%	0.045%	0.121%	-0.491%	-1.054%	0.050%
			(-1.9)	(1.3)	(0.6)	(-0.4)	(0.9)	(0.9)	(-1.2)	(-3.6)	-
		N	11	7	5	7	6	13	30	37	1

D. *Support vector machines*

In this study, we use a SVM, which is one of various types of learning models commonly used for predicting prices. SVMs use a Gaussian kernel function [15]. The Gaussian function has two settings, parameter σ^2 and slack coefficients, which are important factors in measuring the superiority of SVMs. We also present our analysis of these parameters here.

$$y = \beta + \Sigma\alpha \; y \; K(x(i), x). \tag{6}$$

E. *Analytical data*

In this section, we summarize the results of our analysis of corporate bond price predictability in the Japanese market. As was confirmed in the previous section, when assessing CERs, fluctuations in corporate bond excess returns are generally small. Therefore, it is more important to be able to predict a large negative excess return as seen in 2009, rather than predicting a positive excess return.

Therefore, in this section, we will focus on predicting the negative excess returns on corporate bonds seen in 2009 by designating the training sample as the period from 2002 to 2008, and the prediction sample as 2009.

When predicting abnormal negative excess returns using a SVM, the CER needs to be classified into two types. Specifically, it is assumed that CERs (+1, +30) are divided into two types with -0.01% as a threshold value, where CERs exceeding -0.01% are defined as normal returns, and CERs of -0.01% or less are defined as abnormal negative returns.

$$R(i) = \text{Normal return if } CER(+1,+30) > -0.01\%, \quad \text{Otherwise, abnormal negative return.} \tag{7}$$

F. *Explanatory variables*

1) *Current net earnings*

One representative data point disclosed in a financial report is current net earnings. Reference [3] states that of the various types of data disclosed in financial reports, current net earnings may possibly affect bond prices. Thus, in predicting bond prices, we conducted our analysis using current net earnings as an explanatory variable. Equation (8) shows the rate of change in current net earnings per share (A) from the previous term (T-1) to the current term (T). Net earnings per share are treated as current net earnings. If ΔA is positive, current term net earnings increase in comparison to the previous term. If ΔA is negative, current net earnings decline over the previous term.

$$dA(T) = (A(T)-A(T-1)) / A(T-1). \tag{8}$$

2) *Management net earnings forecasts*

Management forecasts of subsequent terms' earnings are announced at the same time as current net earnings in financial results. In research studies using stock prices, it has also been reported that the influence of the manager next term earnings forecast is greater than the impact of current net earnings. In this study, it is assumed that the management earnings forecast is an explanatory variable and analyzed as such [9]. In our analysis, we focus on net earnings forecast per share and investigate its impact on bond prices. Equation (9) shows the rate of change in net earnings per share (A) during a specific period (T) and the net earnings forecast by management (F) for the subsequent term (T+1). If ΔF is positive, earnings are expected to increase during the T+1 period compared with net earnings during term T. Conversely, if ΔF is negative, earnings during the T+1 period are expected to be lower than net earnings during term T.

$$dF(T+1) = (F(T+1)-A(T)) / A(T). \tag{9}$$

3) *Index of business conditions*

Reference [3] states that bond price responses may differ depending on the business conditions during the fiscal year that financial results are announced. This study uses two indices, a composite index (CI) and a diffusion index (DI), as indicators capturing the economic trends in this study's sample period 2002 to 2010. The CI measures the magnitude of economic fluctuations and their tempo by compiling the movements of component indicators, while the DI calculates the proportion of these indicators that have exhibited improvement in order to measure diffusion to each component of the economy. There are three types of indices that make up the CI and DI: the leading index that precedes the economic condition, the coincident index that moves in concert with the economy, and the lagging index that moves after (lags) the economic condition. We use the coincident index to understand the current condition of the economy, and because the leading index generally precedes the coincident index by several months, we use this to predict the future movement in the economy. In general, the lagging index lags the coincident index by about a half year, so it is used for ex post factual confirmation.

4) Ratings

Ratings are commonly used as indicators of the financial condition of a company. Reference [3] found that in addition to the impact of financial report data on bond prices, bond prices could also be impacted by ratings and decline significantly when these ratings are low.

While there are five rating agencies, R&I, the Japan Credit Rating Agency (JCR), Standard & Poor's (S&P), Moody's, and Fitch, for this analysis, we adopted R&I, which has the highest coverage rate for our samples.

III. ANALYSIS RESULTS

In this section, we describe how we modeled corporate bond price predictions using a SVM. We analyze the differences between the explanatory variables, then analyze the adjusted parameters, the impact of different models on the kernel functions, and the cross-validation.

A. *Analysis of differences between explanatory variables*

In this section, we analyze the effects of differences between explanatory variables, which are the current net earnings, management earnings forecasts, ratings, and index of business conditions, as explained in Section II above. Reference [3] indicates that it is possible that corporate bond prices may have a particular impact on current net earnings. Therefore, we add other variables under the assumption that current net earnings were already added.

Using the training data, we look into the suitability of our model based on differences in the explanatory power of the variables for bond prices. First, by combining current net earnings, ratings, and the index of business conditions (six patterns) and looking at the fit for the training model, we can see that a high hit ratio is achieved for all combinations. In particular, the highest hit ratio is for the combination of current net earnings, ratings, and coincident CI at 84.66%. In considering the six trends in the index of business conditions, we can conclude that the CI is more suitable than the DI. Because the CI represents the magnitude and tempo of economic fluctuations and the DI represents the degree of economic diffusion, there is a possibility that corporate bond prices are affected by both the magnitude of economic fluctuations as well as their tempo.

Next, by combining the three variables of management earnings forecasts, ratings, and the index of business conditions (six patterns) and observing the fit for the training model, we can also find that a high hit ratio can be achieved for all combinations of these variables as well. In particular, the hit ratio generated increased to 83.82% when a coincident CI was used. In addition, by comparing the fitness of the six patterns of the index of business conditions, it can be concluded that the CI is more suitable than the DI. The same trend can be observed when using current net earnings and ratings as explanatory variables.

Next, we can find that the hit ratio can reach as high as 78.64% when observing the degree of fitness for the training model exhibited by the three variables of current net earnings, management earnings forecasts, and ratings. This indicates that a certain frequency of correct responses can be obtained only by using the combination of current net earnings, management earnings forecasts, and ratings, even when the index of business conditions is not included in the explanatory variables.

Last, when combining the four variables of current net earnings, management earnings forecasts, ratings, and index of business conditions (six patterns), we found that a high hit ratio is achieved for all combinations. Specifically, we found that the hit ratio was highest when using a coincident CI, at 84.66%.

TABLE III. THE PREDICTION PERFORMANCE OF VARIABLE DIFFERENCES FOR TRAINING DATA

Number of Variable	Variables[a]		Training Data: Number of Hit /Total Number	Training Data: Hit Ratio
3	NE,	R, Leading CI	985/1193	82.56%
	NE,	R, Coincident CI	1010/1193	84.66%
	NE,	R, Lagging CI	962/1193	80.64%
	NE,	R, Leading DI	955/1193	80.05%
	NE,	R, Coincident DI	936/1193	78.46%
	NE,	R, Lagging DI	936/1193	78.46%
	EF,	R, Leading CI	985/1193	82.56%
	EF,	R, Coincident CI	1000/1193	83.82%
	EF,	R, Lagging CI	957/1193	80.22%
	EF,	R, Leading DI	964/1193	80.80%
	EF,	R, Coincident DI	933/1193	78.21%
	EF,	R, Lagging DI	933/1193	78.21%
	NE,EF,	R	936/1193	78.46%
4	NE,EF,	R, Leading CI	984/1193	82.48%
	NE,EF,	R, Coincident CI	1010/1193	84.66%
	NE,EF,	R, Lagging CI	963/1193	80.72%
	NE,EF,	R, Leading DI	946/1193	79.30%
	NE,EF,	R, Coincident DI	941/1193	78.88%
	NE,EF,	R, Lagging DI	936/1193	78.46%

a. NE: Current Net Earnings, EF: Earning Forecast, R: Rating.

Next, we look at the prediction performance for holdout data. First, when looking at the prediction results when the three variables of current net earnings, ratings, and index of business conditions (six patterns) are combined, the hit ratio when using a leading CI or a coincident CI is very high at 97.86% for abnormal negative returns, and very low for normal returns, at 5.41%. In contrast, when using other indices of business conditions, we find that the hit ratio for normal returns is high and the hit ratio for abnormal negative returns is very low. This suggests that the training model may be overfitting.

Next, looking at the prediction results when using a combination of the three variables of management earnings forecasts, ratings, and the index of business conditions (six patterns), use of the leading CI and the coincident CI resulted in a high hit ratio for abnormal negative returns of 80.61% and 97.96%, respectively, but the hit ratio for normal returns was low. In contrast, when using other indices of business conditions, we find that the hit ratio for normal returns is high and the hit ratio for abnormal negative returns is very low. This suggests the possibility that the training model may be overfitting, similar to what occurs using current net earnings.

Next, when assessing the prediction results when using the three variables of current net earnings, management earnings forecasts, and ratings, the hit ratio for abnormal negative returns is 0, and the hit ratio for normal returns is 94.59%. There is a possibility that the training model is overfitting in this case as well.

Finally, in assessing prediction results when using a combination of the four variables of current net earnings, management earnings forecasts, ratings, and the index of business conditions (six patterns), the hit ratio when using a leading CI is 89.13% for abnormal negative returns, and 29.73% for normal returns. Although the hit ratio for normal returns is not high, there is a possibility that the hit ratio could be improved by adjusting parameters. Results from using other indices of business conditions appear to be strongly biased towards either abnormal negative returns or normal returns, suggesting the possibility of overfitting by the training model.

In this section, we analyze the effects of the differences in the explanatory variables used, and as a result, we find that the highest predictability for corporate bond prices is achieved when using the four explanatory variables of current net earnings, management earnings forecasts, ratings, and the leading CI.

TABLE IV. THE PREDICTION PERFORMANCE OF VARIABLE DIFFERENCES FOR HOLDOUT DATA

Number of Variable	Variables[a]		Holdout Data: Abnormal Negative Return: Number of Hit /Total Number	Hit Ratio	Normal Return: Number of hit /Total Number	Hit Ratio
3	NE,	R, Leading CI	96/98	97.96%	2/37	5.41%
	NE,	R, Coincident CI	96/98	97.96%	0/37	0.00%
	NE,	R, Lagging CI	5/98	5.10%	31/37	83.78%
	NE,	R, Leading DI	0/98	0.00%	35/37	94.59%
	NE,	R, Coincident DI	0/98	0.00%	35/37	94.59%
	NE,	R, Lagging DI	0/98	0.00%	35/37	94.59%
	EF,	R, Leading CI	79/98	80.61%	12/37	32.43%
	EF,	R, Coincident CI	96/98	97.96%	0/37	0.00%
	EF,	R, Lagging CI	1/98	1.02%	37/37	100.00%
	EF,	R, Leading DI	3/98	3.06%	37/37	100.00%
	EF,	R, Coincident DI	0/98	0.00%	37/37	100.00%
	EF,	R, Lagging DI	0/98	0.00%	37/37	100.00%
	NE,EF,	R	0/98	0.00%	35/37	94.59%
4	NE,EF,	R, Leading CI	88/98	89.80%	11/37	29.73%
	NE,EF,	R, Coincident CI	96/98	97.96%	0/37	0.00%
	NE,EF,	R, Lagging CI	16/98	16.33%	30/37	81.08%
	NE,EF,	R, Leading DI	0/98	0.00%	2/37	5.41%
	NE,EF,	R, Coincident DI	0/98	0.00%	37/37	100.00%
	NE,EF,	R, Lagging DI	0/98	0.00%	37/37	100.00%

a. NE: Current Net Earnings, EF: Earning Forecast, R: Rating.

B. *Analysis of parameter differences*

In the previous section, we analyzed the differences between variables, and as a result, found that the best case arises when making corporate bond price predictions using the four variables of current net earnings, management earnings forecasts, ratings, and the leading CI. We then determined the most suitable parameters assuming these four variables.

The SVM has two parameters: one the variance σ^2 of the kernel function (Gaussian) and the other the slack coefficient representing the degree of relaxation of the constraining condition when the discrimination is not possible. By adjusting these two parameters, we are able to look at the suitability for our model.

First, we analyze the hit ratio from the training data and the holdout data after fixing the slack coefficients and the kernel function parameters adjusted from 0.6 to 1. The hit ratio for the training data exceeded 80% in all cases, resulting in a high hit ratio. On the other hand, for the hit ratio for the holdout data, utilized a lower kernel function parameter, as the hit ratio for abnormal negative returns tended to decrease, the hit ratio for normal returns tended to increase. Overall, the hit ratios of abnormal negative returns and normal returns both exceeded 60% when the parameter of the kernel function was set to 0.6.

We next looked at the hit ratio for the training and holdout data after adjusting the kernel function parameter to 0.6 and changing the slack coefficient from 0.5 to 2. The difference in the hit ratio for the training data was not much despite adjusting the slack coefficient, and exceeded 80% in all cases. In contrast, for the hit ratio for the holdout data, which utilized a lower slack coefficient, as the hit ratio for abnormal negative returns tended to decrease, the hit ratio for the normal return tended to increase. In particular, correct responses for both abnormal negative returns and the normal returns exceeded 60% when the slack coefficient was 1.0.

TABLE V. THE PREDCTIONS PERFORMANCE OF PARAMETER DIFFERENCES FOR TRAINING DATA

Variables[a]	Parameter	Slack Coefficient	Training Data: Number of Hit /Total Number	Hit Ratio
NE,EF,R,Leading CI	1	1	984/1193	82.48%
	0.5	1	980/1193	82.15%
	0.75	1	986/1193	82.65%
	0.9	1	986/1193	82.65%
	0.6	1	975/1193	81.73%
	0.6	2	989/1193	82.90%
	0.6	0.5	957/1193	80.22%

a. NE: Current Net Earnings, EF: Earning Forecast, R: Rating.

TABLE VI. THE PREDICTION PERFORMANCE OF PARAMETER DIFFERENCES FOR HOLDOUT DATA

Variables[a]	Parameter	Slack Coefficient	Holdout Data: Abnormal Negative Return: Number of Hit /Total Number	Hit Ratio	Normal Return: Number of Hit /Total Number	Hit Ratio
NE,EF,R,Leading CI	1	1	88/98	89.80%	11/37	29.73%
	0.5	1	53/98	54.08%	27/37	72.97%
	0.75	1	73/98	74.49%	17/37	45.95%
	0.9	1	77/98	78.57%	15/37	40.54%
	0.6	1	64/98	65.31%	23/37	62.16%
	0.6	2	77/98	78.57%	12/37	32.43%
	0.6	0.5	37/98	37.76%	30/37	81.08%

a. NE: Current Net Earnings, EF: Earning Forecast, R: Rating.

In this section, we analyze differences in parameters and predict the movement of corporate bond prices using the four variables of current net earnings, management earnings forecasts, ratings, and the leading CI. We find that the model fits best when using a kernel function (Gaussian) with a parameter of 0.6 and a slack coefficient of 1.0.

C. *Analysis using different Kernel functions*

In this analysis, we use the Gaussian function as a general SVM kernel function. In this section, we summarize the results of our analysis of each of three different kernel functions; the linear, polynomial, and sigmoid, other than the Gaussian function, fit with our model.

First, we set the parameters of each kernel function to 1, and then observed the hit ratio for the training data. However, as the hit ratio was low, we changed the parameters and checked the hit ratio again. As a result of the changes, the hit ratio for the training data achieved a 70% range for all kernel functions, lower than the 80% level achieved using the Gaussian function.

The parameters for each Kernel function were adjusted and we looked into the prediction performance for holdout data. As a result, the hit ratio for normal returns increased with all kernel functions, while the hit ratio for abnormal negative returns was as low as the 30% range. Based on these results, we concluded that the Gaussian function is the most suitable for predicting abnormal negative returns.

In this section, by checking the hit ratio for corporate bond prices due to the differences in the SVM kernel functions, we found that the Gaussian function is the most suitable function among the Gaussian, linear, polynomial, and sigmoid functions tested.

TABLE VII. THE PREDICTION PERFORMANCE OF DIFFERENT KERNEL FUNCTIONS FOR TRAINING DATA

Kernel	Parameter	Training Data	
		Number of Hit /Total Number	Hit Ratio
Liner	0.6	933/1193	78.21%
Polynominal	0.6	879/1193	73.68%
Polynominal	0.1	900/1193	75.44%
Sigmoid	0.6	849/1193	71.17%
Sigmoid	0.1	850/1193	71.25%
Sigmoid	2	850/1193	71.25%

TABLE VIII. THE PREDICTION PERFORMANCE OF DIFFERENT KERNEL FUNCTIONS FOR HOLDOUT DATA

Kernel	Parameter	Holdout Data			
		Abnormal Negative Return		Normal Return	
		Number of Hit /Total Number	Hit Ratio	Number of Hit /Total Number	Hit Ratio
Liner	0.6	0/98	0.00%	37/37	100.00%
Polynominal	0.6	38/98	38.78%	24/37	64.86%
Polynominal	0.1	38/98	38.78%	24/37	64.86%
Sigmoid	0.6	38/98	38.78%	24/37	64.86%
Sigmoid	0.1	38/98	38.78%	24/37	64.86%
Sigmoid	2	33/98	33.67%	24/37	64.86%

D. *Analysis of cross-validation*

The issue of model overlearning has been highlighted in regard to constructive learning models. Therefore, in this section, we summarize our findings when checking for overfitting in our training model using k-fold cross-validation.

Here, we analyze the cross-validation under the conditions tested among the various analyses conducted previously that resulted in the highest rates of correct responses by the training model and prediction model. Specifically, when we predict the movements of corporate bond prices using the four variables of current net earnings, management earnings forecasts, ratings, and the leading CI, we used the Gaussian kernel function with a parameter of 0.6 and a slack coefficient of 1.0. The division method used consisted of separating the data into 10 groups during the 2002 to 2008 training period.

In viewing the results, the hit ratio on cross validation is as high as 80.1%. From this, it seems that such a result indicates that it is highly likely that the model in this study is not overfitting.

IV. CONCLUSION AND FUTURE WORK

In this study, we analyze the predictability of corporate bond prices following company announcements of financial results using a SVM.

From our analysis, we find that we are able to obtain (1) the highest prediction performance when using the four variables of current net earnings, management earnings forecasts, ratings, and the leading CI, and (2) the highest prediction performance when using a Gaussian kernel function with a parameter of 0.6 and a slack coefficient of 1.0 as model conditions.

These results offer captivating insights regarding the predictability of prices in the corporate bond market using a SVM.

In terms of future work, we plan to expand the data to current year and to apply the same structure to other bond markets outside of Japan.

REFERENCES

[1] H. Jotaki,S. Takahashi,H. Takahashi,"The Impact of Headline News on Credit Market in Japan", Nippon Finance Association 17th conference, pp. 113-122, 2009

[2] H. Jotaki,Y. Yamashita,H. Takahashi "The Impact of M&A on the corporate bond Market in Japan —From the point of view of fixed income investment —", Market Structure Analysis and New asset management method, Japanese Association of Financial Econometrics and Engineering Journal, pp. 56-74, 2012.

[3] H. Jotaki,Y. Yamashita,H. Takahashi,"The effect of earing announcement on corporate bond market in Japan", Market Structure Analysis and New asset management method, Japanese Association of Financial Econometrics and Engineering Journal, pp. 56-74, 2012.

[4] G. Levent, H. Dirk,"Corporate bond credit spreads and forecast dispersion", Journal of Banking & Finance, vol. 34, pp. 2328-2345, 2010.

[5] P. Collin-Dufresne, R. Goldstein, and J. Martin, "The determinants of credit spread changes" Journal of Finance, vol. 60, pp. 2255-2281, Dec. 2001.

[6] E. Fama "Efficient Capital Markets: A Review of Theory and Empirical Work", The Journal of Finance, vol. 25,pp. 383-417, 1970.

[7] F. Sharpe, "Capital Asset Prices:A Theory of Market Equilibrium under condition of Risk", The Journal of Finance, vol. 19, pp. 425-442, 1964.

[8] K. Ota, "Reaction comparison of TSE part, TSE II, Osaka, and over-the-counter markets for financial announcement", Kansai University Graduate School Senriyama Commerce, 53, 2001.

[9] R. Conroy,K. Harris,and Y. Park,"Fundamental information and share prices in Japan: Evidence from earnings surprises and management predictions", International Journal of Forecasting, vol. 14, no. 2, pp. 227-244, June 1998.

[10] R. Conroy. K. Eades,and T. Harris,"A test of the relative pricing effect of dividend and earnings : Evidence from simultaneous announcements in Japan", The Journal of Finance, vol. 55, pp. 1199-1227, 2000.

[11] D. Hon,P. Padhy,"Support Vector Machines for Prediction of Futures Prices in Indian Stock Market", International Journal of Computer Applications, vol. 41. no. 3, March 2012.

[12] K. Kyoung-jae Kim, "Financial time series forecasting using support vector machines", Neurocomputing, vol. 55, pp. 307-319, 2003.

[13] A. Warge,W.Ivo,"Bondholder losses in leveraged buyouts", Review of Financial Studies, vol. 6, pp. 959-982, 1993.

[14] M. Billett, T. King, and D. Mauer, "Bondholder wealth effects in mergers and acquisitions: New evidence from the 1980s and 1990s", Journal of Finance, vol. 59, pp. 107-135, Feb. 2004.

[15] M. Buhmann, "Radial basis function", Mathematicshes Institut, Justus-Liebig-Universitat Giessen, 2010.

Automatic Text Summarization: A review

Naima Zerari, Samia Aitouche, Mohamed Djamel Mouss, Asma Yaha
Automation and Manufacturing Laboratory
Department of Industrial Engineering
Batna 2 University
Batna, Algeria
Email: n.zerari@yahoo.fr, samiaaitouche@yahoo.fr, d_mouss@yahoo.fr, yahaasma@gmail.com

***Abstract*—As we move into the 21st century, with very rapid mobile communication and access to vast stores of information, we seem to be surrounded by more and more information, with less and less time or ability to digest it. The creation of the automatic summarization was really a genius human solution to solve this complicated problem. However, the application of this solution was too complex. In reality, there are many problems that need to be addressed before the promises of automatic text summarization can be fully realized. Basically, it is necessary to understand how humans summarize the text and then build the system based on that. Yet, individuals are so different in their thinking and interpretation that it is hard to create "gold-standard" summary against which output summaries will be evaluated. In this paper, we will discuss the basic concepts of this topic by giving the most relevant definitions, characterizations, types and the two different approaches of automatic text summarization: extraction and abstraction. Special attention is devoted to the extractive approach. It consists of selecting important sentences and paragraphs from the original text and concatenating them into shorter form. Broadly, the importance of sentences is decided based on statistical features of sentences. This approach avoids any efforts on deep text understanding. It is conceptually simple and easy to implement.**

Keywords- Text summarization; Automatic text summarization; Abstractive approach; Extractive approach; Natural language processing.

I. INTRODUCTION

The rapid evolution of WWW has made huge quantity of documents on a variety of topics available to the users [1][2]. To exploit these documents effectively, it is required to be able to get a summary of them. However, it is very difficult for humans to create a hand written summary of the entire available document. Automatic Text Summarization (ATS) provides a solution to this information overload problem [2]. Hence, ATS has become an important and timely tool for user to quickly understand the large volume of information [3]. The automatic summarization included in language processing field, is the process of dealing with a large amount of information by comprising only the essential ones. It often occurs in everyday communication and it is an important and professional skill for some people. Automatic text summarization aims at providing a condensed representation of the content according to the information that the user wants to get [4]. With document summary available, users can easily decide its relevancy to their interests and acquire desired documents with much less mental loads involved. [5].

Furthermore, the goal of automatic text summarization is to condense the documents into a shorter version and preserve important contents [3]. Text Summarization methods can be classified into two major methods extractive and abstractive summarization [6].

The rest of the paper is organized as follows: Section 2 is about text summarization, precisely the definition of the summary; Section 3 describes the automatic text summarization; Section 4 depicts the models of automatic text summarization; Section 5 defines the summaries characteristics; Section 6 presents a brief review of the two text summarization methods and finally Section 7 concludes this paper and outlines the envisaged research work.

II. TEXT SUMMARIZATION

The human being needs a summary mainly because it reduces reading time and it makes the selection process easier during the search of document process.

Text summarization can be used by various applications; for instance researchers need a summary for deciding whether to read the entire document or not and for summarizing information searched by user on Internet. Summarizing documents involves cognitive effort from the summarizer: different fragments of a text must be selected, reformulated and assembled according to their relevance. The coherence of the information included in the summary must also be taken into account [7]. Thus, text summarization, the reduction of a text to its essential content, is a task that requires linguistic competence, world knowledge, and intelligence [7]. The subfield of summarization has been investigated by the Natural Language Processing (NLP) community for nearly the last half century. Radev et al [8] define a summary as: “a text that is produced from one or more texts that convey important information in the original text, and that is no longer than half of the original text(s) and usually significantly less than that”. This simple definition captures three important aspects that characterize research on automatic summarization [8]:

- Summaries may be produced from a single document or multiple documents.
- Summaries should preserve important information.
- Summaries should be short.

The summary done by means of a computer, i.e., automatically, is called Automatic Text Summarization.

III. AUTOMATIC TEXT SUMMARIZATION

Automatic text summarization is the technique which compresses a large text to a shorter text which includes the important information. The computer program is given a text and it returns a summary of the original text. This is done by reducing redundancy of the text and by extracting the essence of the text [9]. Generally, a summary should be much shorter than the source text. This characteristic is defined by the compression rate, which measures the ratio of length of summary to the length of original text [3]. The first effort on automatic text summarization system was made in the late 1950. This automatic summarizer selects significant sentences from the document and concatenates them together [3]. Currently automatic text summarization has benefited from the expertise of a range of fields of research: information retrieval and information extraction, natural language generation, discourse studies, machine learning and technical studies used by professional summarizers [7]. Summaries can be divided in two main categories: extractive and abstractive.

An abstractive summarization tries to develop an understanding of the main concepts in a document and then express those concepts in clear natural language. It uses linguistic methods to study the text and then to find the new concepts and expressions to best describe it by generating a new shorter text that conveys the salient information from the original text document [6]. This method is the more difficult and it is poorly practical. It is highly complex as it needs extensive natural language processing.

An extractive summarization consists of selecting important sentences or paragraphs from the original document and concatenating them into shorter form. The importance of sentences is decided based on statistical and linguistic features of sentences [6]. This method is fairly applicable and it usually gives reasonable result. Therefore research community is focusing more on extractive summaries, trying to achieve more coherent and meaning full summaries. Several work have been presented in this context such as: Othman et al. [10] who described the contributions made in text summarization field and presented a comparative study of Text Summarization Techniques. Gupta and Lehal [6] presented a survey of Text Summarization, extractive techniques, specifying that the biggest challenge for text summarization, is to summarize content from a number of textual and semi structured sources, including databases and web pages, in the right way. Saranyamol and Sindhu [11] presented a survey describing different approaches of the automatic text summarization process and made an analysis of different methods. Khan and Salim [3] proposed a survey on abstractive text summarization methods and concluded that most of the abstractive summarization methods produce highly coherent, cohesive, rich information and less redundant summary. Munot and Govilkar [12] discussed in details the two main categories of text summarization methods and also presented a taxonomy of summarization systems, statistical and linguistic approaches for summarization. Sariki et al [2] proposed a system to generate a summary of a single document, specifying the keywords and adjusting the length of the final summary to produce. The proposed system has been improved a lot in accuracy. The authors precise also that the generated summary can be visualized in the form of a Power Point presentation (PPT), thus making it easy for the user to create an effective classroom presentation. So, they propose to extend their work to multiple documents in future. Chandra et al [5] proposed K-mixture semantic relationship significance (KSRS) approach. It is a statistical approach to text summarization. The proposed approach combines the K- mixture term weighting scheme, based on a mathematical (probabilistic) ground, and the linguistic technique. This latter explores term relationships by finding the semantic relationship significance of nouns that signifies term and sentence semantics. The authors specified that the proposed approach, KSRS, performs better and consequently its feasibility in text summarization applications is justifiable. Also, they specified that its use allows the choice of a lower summary proportion without worrying about the performance deterioration.

IV. AUTOMATIC TEXT SUMMARIZATION MODELS

Depending upon the number of documents accepted as input by a summarization process, automatic text summarization can be categorized as single document summarization and multi-document summarization as shown in Fig. 1 below.

In the model Single Document Text Summarization, a summary is produced from single input document. The single document summarization process flow can be depicted in Fig. 2. However, in Multi Document Text Summarization, a summary is produced from multiple input documents dealing with the same topic as illustrate in Fig. 3. In 1995, Radev and McKeown [13] were the first to develop a system for generating summaries of multiple documents. Multidocument summarization is one of the major challenges in current summarization systems because the task of summarizing multiple documents is more difficult than the task of summarizing single documents where the redundancy [1] is the main problems in summarizing multiple documents.

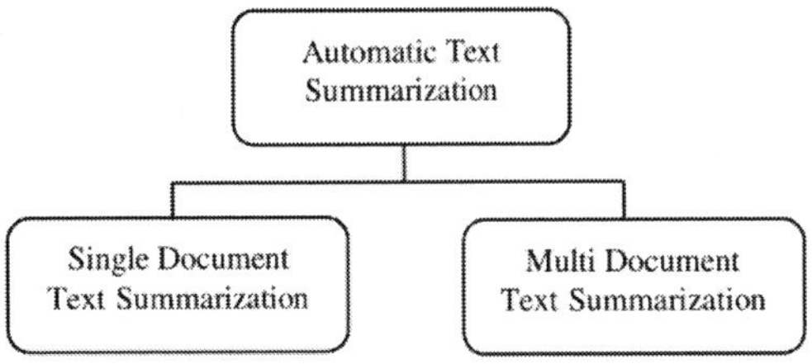

Figure 1. Automatic Text Summarization Models

V. Characteristics of Summaries

The summary is characterized by various features cited below [8]:

1. Language: designates the language of the input; it can be monolingual or multilingual.
2. Genre: represents scientific article, report, news or other.
3. Type of document: specifies the type of the document used as an input; it can be classified into two types:
   a. Single document summarizes: creates a summary from one document.
   b. Multiple documents summary: creates a summary from a number of related documents summarization (more than one document). The distinct characteristic that makes multi document summarization rather different from single document is the use of multiple sources of information that overlap and supplement each other, being contradictory. So the fundamental tasks do not consist just on identifying and coping with redundancy across documents, but also ensuring that the final summary is both coherent and complete.
4. Domain: Corresponds to the domain of summarization such as science, technology, literature, law, etc. It is defined by two types:
   a. Restricted summary: provides summary on restricted domain.
   b. Unrestricted summary: applies for all type of documents. So, there is not dependence on the domain and can be used by any type of user.
5. Type of information: Signifies the type of information used, it encloses two types:
   a. Background information: teaches about the topic.
   b. New information summary: provides just the newest facts, assuming the reader is familiar with the topic.
6. Audience: designates the method used to write a summary, defined by two types:
   a. Generic summary: provides the author's point of view. Generic summarization purpose is to summarize all texts regardless of its topic or domain; i.e., generic summaries make no assumptions about the domain of its source information and view all documents as homogenous texts [14].
   b. Query based summary: focuses on material of interest to the user.
7. Function: Signifies the type of the function used to transform the document to a summary, and it covers three types:
   a. Informative summary: reflects the content of the original text.
   b. Indicative summary: merely provides an indication of what the original text was about.
   c. Evaluative summary: evaluates the subject matter of the source, expressing the abstractor's views on the quality of the work of the author.

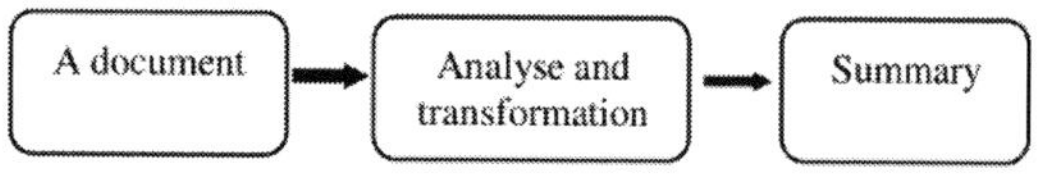

Figure2. Single Document Text Summarization

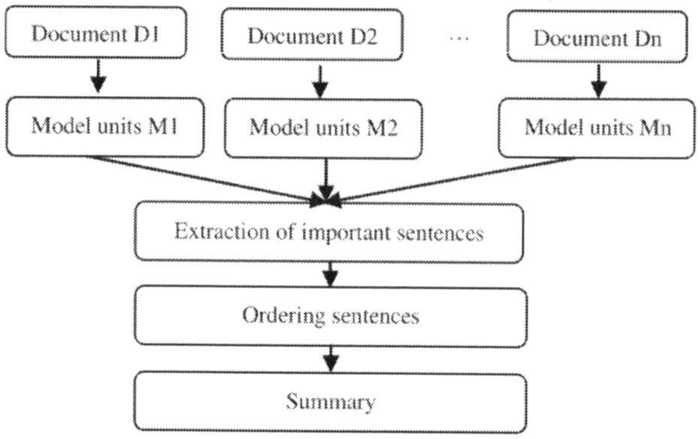

Figure3. Multi Document Text Summarization

VI. Methods of Summarizing

The output of summary can be of two types: Extractive summaries and Abstractive summaries. Extractive summaries are produced by extracting the whole sentences from the source text. The importance of sentences is determined based on statistical and linguistic features of sentences [9]. Abstractive summaries are produced by reformulating sentences of the source text. The principle of abstractive summarizer consists to understand the main concepts in a document and then convey those concepts in clear natural language. It uses linguistic methods to examine and interpret the text and then to find the new concepts and terms to best describe it by generating new shorter text that conveys the most significant information from the original text document [9].

A. Extractive Method

Extractive approach purpose is to create the summary by extracting the important sentences from the original document [2]. The extracted sentences will be then grouped to produce a summary with maintaining the order as in the original document and without changing the source text [11]. Most of the work in text summarization has focused on extractive summarization because it is conceptually simple and easy to be implemented. Generally, there are three types of approach to extract sentences in summary generation: the statistical, the linguistic and machine learning approach [10].

1) Linguistic Approach

This technique involves knowledge of the language so that the computer can analyze the sentences semantically and then decide what sentences to choose considering the position of the subject, verb and the noun [10]. It is more difficult than statistical methods.

2) Machine Learning Approach

A Machine Learning (ML) approach is useful where a collection of documents and their corresponding reference extractive summaries are available [15]. The ML aims at learning from a training model in order to determine the appropriate class where an element belongs to. The sentences of each document will be representing by means of vectors of features extracted from the text [15][14]. Thus, the goal of training model is to classify sentences in two categories: sentence labelled as "summary sentence" when it belong to the reference summary or as "non-summary sentence" other than. This process of learning from the collection of documents and its summaries allow the use of the trained model to produce an extractive summary when a new document is given to the system [14]. Some ML methods used for single document will be described.

A. Text Summarization with Neural Networks

This method involves neural network training to identify the type of sentences that must be inserted in the summary. The neural network learns the patterns that are essential in sentences and that should be included in the summary. Generally, this method uses Feed forward neural network architecture with three layers [11].

B. Text Summarization with Naive Bayes

One of the early works that integrated machine learning was the use of Naive Bayes classifier for learning from the data in 1995 [14]. In this method, the classification function namely naïve- bayes is used to categorize_each sentence as worthy of extraction or not [16][17].

3) Statistical Approach

In Statistical technique, the summary is created without understanding, but rather depends on the statistical distribution of certain properties [10]. This technique aims at deriving weights of key terms and determine the sentence importance by the total weight the sentence contains [5].

- *Statistical Technique Steps*

The statistical technique is realized in the following different steps:

a. Pre-processing
b. Analyzing

a. Pre-processing: is the initial step of loading the given text into the proposed system and decomposing it into its constituent sentences (takes a raw text as an input and applies some basic routines to transform or eliminate textual elements that are not useful in further processing of textual data). Normalization is the method of converting the text into normalized form by performing processes, such as case-folding, tokenization, stop word removal and stemming. Thus, the Pre-Processing steps are [2][18]:

- Case-folding ;
- Tokenization ;
- Stop word removal ;
- Stemming.

▪ Case-Folding: is the process of converting the given text into lower case text in order to avoid repetition of the same word in different cases. This helps the system to distinguish similar terms and improves its accuracy [2][18].

▪ Tokenization: is the process of splitting text into sentence and each sentence into words. For sentence segmentation, dot is taken as separator and for words space is taken into account [2][18].

▪ Stop word removal: is the process of removing the stop words, i.e., words which are of less semantic information. Words which are very common and occur in a large majority of the documents but do not include much semantic information are termed as stop words, such as: "the", "by", "a", "an", etc.

Categorization is only based on feature terms and not on full stops, commas, colons, semicolons, etc. So they are removed from the document and will not be stored in the signature file for further process [2][18].

Stemming: The objective of this process is to obtain the stem or radix of each word (in general, a text document contains repetitions of the same word with variations), which emphasize its semantics [15]. It deals with syntactically-similar words, such as plurals, verbal variations, etc. [15]. The purpose of this procedure is to obtain the stem or radix of each word, which emphasize its semantics [15]. Stemming can be of two types [2]:

- Derivational Stemming.
- Inflectional Stemming.

Derivational stemming creates new words from existing words, e.g., "Finalize-Final", "Useful-Use", "Musical-Music", etc. However, Inflectional stemming confines normalized words to grammatical variants like past tense or present tense or singular or plural form, e.g., "Management-Manage", "Classification-Classify", "Payment-Pay", etc. [2][18].

b. Analyzing: This stage has traditionally been decomposed into three steps [2][18]:

- Ranking: Conception of the structure of analyzing using to summarize.
- Selection: Transformation by using a function "Statistic function".
- Ordering: ordering the new statements for make an understandable summary.

- *Methods of Statistical Technique*

Scoring is the process of assigning a score for each sentence to determine its importance in the summary [2]. Text summarization identifies and extracts key sentences from the source text and concatenates them to form a concise summary. Importance of a sentence can be decided by several methods, such as:

- *TF-IDF method (Term Frequency-Inverse Document Frequency)*

This method introduced in 1989 [19]. The term frequency (TF) contributes to the similarity strength as the number of word occurrences is higher. Whereas, the inverse document frequency (IDF) regards low frequency words inversely contributes to higher value to the measurement [19]. The purpose of tf-idf is to reduce the weightage of frequent occurring words by comparing its proportional frequency in the document collection. This property has made the tf-idf to be one of the commonly used terminologies in extractive summarization [14].

- Cue-Phrase Method

Words that would have positive or negative effect on the respective sentence weight to indicate significance or key idea [3], such as cues: "in summary", "in conclusion", "the paper describes", "significantly".

- Title Method

This method states that sentences that appear in the title are considered to be more important and are more likely to be included in the summary. The score of the sentences is calculated as how many words are commonly used between a sentence and a title. Title method cannot be effective if the document does not include any title information [12].

- Location Method

It relies on the intuition that important sentences are located at certain position in text or in paragraph, such as beginning or end of a paragraph [3]. Therefore, important information in a document is often covered by writers at the beginning of the article. Thus the beginning sentences are assumed to contain the most important content [11].

- Sentence length

Very short sentences are usually not included in summary as they convey less information. Very long sentences are also not suitable to represent a summary [20].

- Proper noun

Sentences containing proper noun representing a unique entity suchlike name of a person, organization or location are considered important to the document [20] [14].

B. Abstractive Method

Abstractive text summarization method is intended to produce important information about the document in a new way, by interpreting and examining the source text and then creating a concise summary, closer to what a human might generate. The summary will contain compressed sentences or may include some novel sentences not present explicitly in the original source text [21][22][23]. It produces an organic summary with a logic structure clearer and more accurate as compared to the summaries produced by extractive approach [12]. However, this method is difficult because it uses linguistic approach to understand the original text [12] and needs deep understanding of the NLP tasks. It is broadly classified in two categories: Structured based approach and Semantic based approach [3].

1) Structured Based Approach

Structured based approach encodes most important information from the document(s) through cognitive schemas [3][11]. Different methods can be used by Structured Based Approach, such as Tree based method, Template based method, ontology based method, lead and body phrase method and Rule based method [3] as illustrated in Fig. 4.

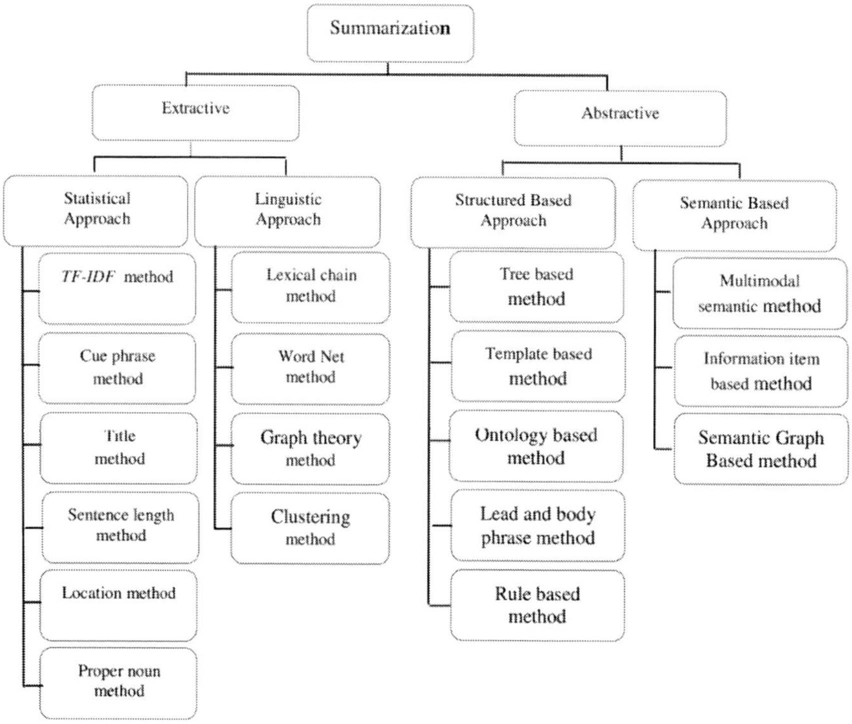

Figure 4. Principles Approaches used in Automatic Text Summarization

2) Semantic Based Approach

In Semantic based approach, a semantic representation of document(s) is used to feed into natural language generation (NLG) system. This method focus on identifying noun phrases and verb phrases by processing linguistic data [3] [11]. Various methods can be used by Structured Based Approach suchlike Multimodal semantic model, Information item based method and Semantic Graph based method [3] as presented in Fig. 4 above.

VII. Conclusion and Future Research

Nowadays, the need of automatic text summarization has augmented due to the rapid increase in number of information on the Internet. Therefore, it is too difficult for users to manually summarize those large online documents. Automatic text summarization solves this problem. It represents one of the natural language processing applications and is becoming more popular for information condensation. It allows getting the important information while dealing with large collection of documents. A good automatic summary captures the essence of a long work in a brief informative statement that can be read and digested quickly. This solution can be developed using either extractive or abstractive approaches that both aimed at analyzing the texts and generalizing summaries. Text summarization by abstractive approach is stronger because it produces summary which is semantically related but difficult to generate. However, text summarization by extractive approach is easier for the human to program and for the computer to understand. This review mainly focused on the fundamental concepts and approaches related to automatic text summarization and its most important characterization. Therefore, much discussion revolves around the extractive approach due to its great use. However, there are a number of limitations pertaining to this approach that is, its sentences can be extracted out of the context and anaphoric references can be broken. Thus, the main aim of this research work is to understand the text summarization process for developing an automatic text summarization system with great accuracy as future work. This objective can be achieved by applying a hybrid method of statistical approach.

Acknowledgment

This research is supported by Automation and Manufacturing Laboratory of Industrial Engineering Department of Batna-2 University.

References

[1] M. Gambhir and V. Gupta, "Recent automatic text summarization techniques : a survey," *Artif. Intell. Rev. Springer Sci. Media Dordr.*, vol. 47, no. 1, pp. 1–66, 2016.

[2] T. P. Sariki, B. Kumar, and R. Ragala, "Effective classroom presentation generation using text summarization," *Comput. Technol. Appl.*, vol. 5, no. August, pp. 1–5, 2014.

[3] A. Khan and Naomie Salim, "A Review On Abstractive Summarization Methos," *J. Theor. Appl. Inf. Technol.*, vol. 59, no. 1, 2014.

[4] F. Kiyoumarsi, "Evaluation of Automatic Text Summarizations based on Human Summaries," *Procedia - Soc. Behav. Sci.*, vol. 192, pp. 83–91, 2015.

[5] M. Chandra, V. Gupta, and S. K. Paul, "A Statistical Approach for Automatic Text Summarization by Extraction," in *International Conference on Communication Systems and Network Technologies*, 2011, pp. 268–271.

[6] V. Gupta, Gurpreet Singh Lehal, and G. S. Lehal, "A Survey of Text Summarization Extractive techniques," *J. Emerg. Technol. Web Intell.*, vol. 2, no. 3, pp. 258–268, 2010.

[7] J.-M. Torres-Moreno, *Automatic Text Summarization*. British Library Cataloguing-in-Publication Data, ISTE Ltd, John Wiley & Sons, Inc., 2014.

[8] D. Das and A. F. Martin, "A Survey on Automatic Text Summarization," *Lit. Surv. Lang. Stat. II course C. 4*, pp. 192–195, 2007.

[9] P. Shah and N. P. Desai, "A Survey of Automatic Text Summarization Techniques for Indian and Foreign Languages," in *International Conference on Electrical, Electronics, and Optimization Techniques (ICEEOT)*, 2016.

[10] B. M. M. Othman, M. Haggag, and M. Belal, "A Taxonomy for Text Summarization," *Inf. Sci. Technol.*, vol. 3, no. 1, pp. 43–50, 2014.

[11] C. S. Saranyamol and L. Sindhu, "A Survey on Automatic Text Summarization," *Int. J. Comput. Sci. Inf. Technol.*, vol. 5, no. 6, pp. 7889–7893, 2014.

[12] N. Munot and S. S. Govilkar, "Comparative Study of Text Summarization Methods," *Int. J. Comput. Appl.*, vol. 102, no. 12, pp. 33–37, 2014.

[13] L. Suanmali and N. Salim, "Literature Reviews for Multi-Document Summarization.", 2008.

[14] Y. J. Kumar, O. S. Goh, H. Basiron, N. H. Choon, and P. C. Suppiah, "A Review on Automatic Text Summarization Approaches," *J. Comput. Sci.*, 2016.

[15] J. Neto, A. Freitas, and C. Kaestner, "Automatic Text Summarization Using a Machine Learning Approach," *Adv. Artif. Intell. Bittencourt, G. G.L. Ramalho, Springer-Verlag Berlin Heidelb.*, pp. 205–215, 2002.

[16] S. Suneetha, "Automatic Text Summarization : The Current State of the art," *Int. J. Sci. Adv. Technol.*, vol. 1, no. 9, pp. 283–293, 2011.

[17] N. Bhatia and A. Jaiswal, "Literature Review on Automatic Text Summarization : Single and Multiple Summarizations," *Int. J. Comput. Appl.*, vol. 117, no. 6, pp. 25–29, 2015.

[18] K. Sarkar, "Sentence Clustering-based Summarization of Multiple Text Documents," *Tech. – Int. J. Comput. Sci. Commun. Technol.*, vol. 2, no. 1, pp. 325–335, 2009.

[19] M. Haque, S. Pervin, and Z. Begum, "Literature Review of Automatic Multiple Documents Text Summarization," *Int. J. Innov. Appl. Stud.*, vol. 3, no. 1, pp. 121–129, 2013.

[20] Y. J. Kumar and N. Salim, "Automatic multi document summarization approaches," *J. Comput. Sci.*, vol. 8, no. 1, pp. 133–140, 2012.

[21] M. Bhide, "Single or Multi-document Summarization Techniques," vol. 4, no. 3, pp. 375–379, 2016.

[22] S. Haiduc, J. Aponte, L. Moreno, and A. Marcus, "On the use of automated text summarization techniques for summarizing source code," *Proc. - Work. Conf. Reverse Eng. WCRE*, pp. 35–44, 2010.

[23] M. S. Patil, M. S. Bewoor, and S. H. Patil, "A Hybrid Approach for Extractive Document Summarization Using Machine Learning and Clustering Technique," *Int. J. Comput. Sci. Inf. Technol.*, vol. 5, no. 2, pp. 1584–1586, 2014.

Keyword Analysis of Intellectual Capital and Knowledge Management in SCOPUS

Aitouche Samia, Laggoune Assia, Titah Mawloud, Mouss Mohamed Djamel, Zerari Naima, Latreche Khaled, Kanit Akila and kanit Abdelghafour, Department of Industrial Engineering, Laboratory of Automation and Manufacturing, University Batna 2, Batna, Algeria

email: samiaaitouche@yahoo.fr, a.laggoun12@yahoo.fr, t.mawloud@yahoo.fr, d_mouss@yahoo.fr, zerari99@yahoo.fr, khaled_lat@yahoo.fr akila.msi2016@gmail.com, k_abdelghafour@yahoo.fr

Abstract— **The aim of this paper is to perform a keyword analysis in two areas of research: Intellectual Capital and Knowledge Management. The keywords are of three types : keywords proposed by the authors in their articles, the keywords that users use in their queries and the densest words existing in a textual corpus. Zipf's law usually applied for natural language is applied in this work for scientifc corpus constituted of confused full articles in each area. We wrote 8 R programs going through titles of articles, authors' keywords, abstracts and full articles to calculate frequencies and interpret them. The keywords of intellectual capital measurement and diclosure have the highest frequencies. The measures are stated by companies in annual reports and could not be integrated in their balance sheets because the classical accounting does not take into acount intellectual capital as an asset. Knowledge management is more oriented towards the capitalization of knowledge to improve business performance and for industries. This work is the first in keyword analysis for the two areas. It could be usefull to prepare glossaries, ontologies and all semantic reasearhes of research areas.**

Keywords-content analysis; keyword analysis; dense word; Zipf's law; intellectual capital; knowledge management.

I. INTRODUCTION

Our work is a quantitative analysis of keywords and in the areas of intellectual capital (IC) and knowledge management (KM). IC focuses on building and governing intellectual assets from strategic and enterprise governance perspectives with some focus on tactics [1]. KM is more detailed and focuses on facilitating and managing knowledge related activities such as creation, capture, transformation and use [1]. Otherwise, they are two faces of the same thing (knowledge); IC capitalizes it to create value and wealth and, KM manages it from acquisition to diffusion.

A set of keywords indexes and densest words in a scientific article are proposed, calculated and analyzed to have an idea on the trends of scientific area via most used and extracted keywords and their evolution in time. In this paper, Zipf's law was applied to confused abstracts of articles of IC and KM. The results were not satisfactory because the size of abstracts' corpus is not sufficient to apply Zipf's law, which is more adapted to larger corpuses. So we applied it on confused full articles of IC and KM separately to try to reach better results.

The gap that we tried to satisfy is the inexistence of keyword analysis in IC and KM. This analysis is limited to articles existing in SCOPUS database and could be extended to other databases in the future.

The paper is structured as follows: Section II contains the related works and Section III designs the solution and the application of R programs for the keyword analysis of IC and KM areas. Section IV is dedicated to analysis of results and finally, possible extensions to the work are announced to conclude the paper in Section V.

II. STATE OF THE ART

In literature, there are several goals to keyword analysis. Among them, there is the research of Jaime I. L. et al [2] which is a proposition of a new keyword search algorithm that takes into account the semantic information extracted from the schemes of the structured and semi-structured data sources. Bang [3] focuses on the disciplines of the journal information system frontiers (ISF) researches. The author created a keyword classification scheme, incorporating new research topics into Barki's information systems keyword classification scheme [24], to describe the disciplines of ISF until 2012, examining word frequency and keyword co-occurrence. This work is limited to one journal in information systems and its results are not generalizable. On the other hand, Choi and Kang [4] extracted manually keywords from abstracts and titles from Journal of Educational Technology (JET) between 1985 and 2013 and found that educational technology research in Korea has been strongly influenced by new media, design theory, and educational assessment. The manual extraction of keywords takes time, limits the sample of articles and statements are true only for the sample; one journal is not sufficient. Wu Bihu et al [5] examine author-selected keywords of research published in Annals of Tourism Research. In total, 5534 keywords from 2504 articles form the basis of this analysis. Iterative coding results in 200 core keywords serving as descriptors of major research subjects, and 10 gene words indicating knowledge domains formed through cross-references and hybridization of core keywords. By employing the social network analysis technique, Gohar and Jacob [6] found that the results highlight the importance of digital media and business, and IT governance to today's information technology management environment.

Zipf's law is used in this work to show how much a scientific text respects it. Zipf stated that if one takes the words making up an extended body of text and ranks them by frequency of occurrence, then the rank of words multiplied by their frequency of occurrence will be approximately constant [7]. In [8], it is shown that the distribution of word frequencies for randomly generated texts is very similar to Zipf's law observed in natural languages such as English. On the internet, Zipf's law appears to be the rule rather than an exception. It is present at the level of routers transmitting data from one geographic location to another and in the content of the World Wide Web [9].

Our work provides a keyword analysis based on the calculation of frequencies of keywords in titles, abstracts and content of scientific articles for IC and KM areas to analyze quantitatively their trends in terms of themes, expressed by these frequencies.

III. Methodology And Data

Databases of research as SCOPUS do not offer keyword analysis and impose the type of exported data files; the performed analyses were adapted accordingly.

A. *Analysed data*

The data is exported from SCOPUS, i.e., a database which indexes thousands of scientific journals and more than fifty millions scientific articles in all areas of research. The data is a set of articles with "intellectual capital" or "knowledge management" in their titles. Analyses were performed on abstracts and full papers (PDF files). The scientific production is higher in KM (10000 articles) than IC (1500 articles), according to data exported on April 16th 2016.

B. *Methodology*

Eight different programs are written in R language to achieve objectives of the study. The algorithms of the frequencies of author's keywords and Zipf's law are presented as examples; they produce results for sections A and E respectively after their implementation. The six remaining programs are developed for the results of B, C and D sections.

Algorithm frequency_authors_keywords

The authors' keywords algorithm contains generic steps

Begin

1- Read the Excel file entries,
2- Separate authors' keywords of that article and put it in a table as they are combined in the same Excel box and separated by semicolons
3- Repeat 1-2 until the Excel file is ended
4- Calculate the frequency of authors' keywords
5- Order by descending order of frequencies
6- Export the ordered Table in Excel
7- Draw the overall graph on years

End.

Algorithm Zipfs_law

The full articles are downloaded and gathered in the same directory to make a text corpus of an area.

Begin

1- Create an Excel file1 containing the names of PDF (acrobat reader) files gathered in a directory, each name in a row,
2- Read the first name of PDF file from the Excel file1 and use it to open the PDF file,
3- Read word by word and write them in text file3 created to include all the content of all PDF files together, and at the end of this operation it will be constituted the corpus of all PDF files (text corpus),
4- Omit the punctuation from the text file3
5- Repeat instructions 2-3 until the Excel file1 is ended,
6- Each word of corpus from text file3 is added in a row in a second Excel file2 without repetition of words,
7 - For each word from Excel file2, calculate frequency of the word in the corpus of text file3
8- Repeat the operations 6-7 until text file3 is ended,
9- Order the Excel file2 in descending order of frequencies
10- For each word from Excel file2, calculate the value of the existing Zipf's law for this word and put it in the second column, using the formula:
Existing Zipf's law (word) = Frequency (word) * rank (word in file2),
11- Calculate the theoretic value of Zipf's law for each word and put it in the third column, only the size of corpus is used as input to the theoretic value using the formula:
Theoretic Zipf's law (word) = Size of the corpus of text file3/rank (word in Excel file2),
12- Repeat 10-11 until the end of Excel file3,
13- Draw the graphs of theoretic and existing Zipf's law
- Note: this algorithm is applied once on IC and once on KM corpuses separately.

End.

IV. Results And Discussion

The analyses were performed on abstracts, full papers and the other items of paper as titles and authors' keywords. In certain cases, papers were analyzed individually then collectively.

A. *Authors' keywords analysis*

1) Authors' keywords analysis in IC area: In Table I, we present the obtained frequencies of the authors' keywords, in descending order (**2308** keywords). The keywords highlited in Table I are discussed.

Table I: Frequencies of Authors' Keywords in IC Area.

Authors' keywords	freq
Intellectual capital management	**865**
Intellectual capital disclosure	860
Intellectual capital statements	850
Intellectual capital reporting	850
Intellectual capital	847
Intellectual capital assets	847
Intellectual capital development	845
Intellectual capital efficiency	839
Intellectual capital redefinition	835
Intellectual capital dimensions	820
Intellectualcapital's components	812
Intellectual capital evaluation	808
Intellectual capital performance	**808**
Intellectual capital of organizations	764
Measuring, management and Reporting Intellectual	**764**
Intellectual capital measurement	**758**

It is noted that research in IC area is oriented more towards **IC management**. At first, accountants are conscious about the measurement of IC as intangible asset and tried to incorporate it to classical balance sheet next to tangible assets, but they have failed. Nowadays, the interest is extended to **managers** trying to disclose and exploit IC to improve business **performance** and IC is reported separately. In addition, it is noted that authors of IC area use a relatively short list of keywords to express the content of their scientific work but with significant frequencies and slight degradation between them. This is explained by the novelty of the field.

2) Authors' keywords analysis in KM area: for KM, the frequencies of authors' keywords are represented in TABLE II, in descending order (**6650** keywords).

TABLE II. FREQUENCIES OF AUTHORS' KEYWORDS IN KM AREA

Authors' keywords	freq	Authors' keywords	freq
knowledge management	**271**	Tacit knowledge	222
Competitive advantage	**253**	information retieval	217
data mining	**252**	knowledge management (KM)	215
knowledge sharing	**252**	Mathematical models	215
humain ressource	**237**	Technology	215
artificial intelligence	236	organisational performance	120
Article	226	**Manufacture**	**119**
world wide web	226	health care	118
strategic planning	222	....	....

It is noted that researches in KM are oriented more toward **KM systems.** The possession of tacit knowledge by experts is a **competitive advantage**. **Data mining** is used for automatic extraction of knowledge from existing databases. **Knowledge sharing** improves collaboration and is a concern of **human resources management** in a business or in a particular production system. The authors' keywords **Manufacture, industrial engineering, industrial economics and cybernetics** are a strong argument that KM systems support industrial engineering and general industry. Moreover, it is noted that the authors of KM use a wide list of keywords relatively to express the content of their scientific work but with less frequencies than those of IC and have rapid degradations in frequencies.

B. *Analysis of users' keywords in the summaries and complete articles*

The purpose of this analysis is to go deeper in the body of articles and search the frequencies of keywords requested by a user (could be scientist) in abstracts or full articles, to choose articles more appropriated to these keywords and incorporate them in his work (e.g. in the form of literature review).

1) Analysis of users' keywords in abstracts of IC area: An individual analysis of articles' abstracts is performed. It is beneficial when the user wishes select an abstract or a group of abstracts to read. The frequencies of users' keywords when analyzing abstracts one by one, vary from an abstract to another and from keyword to another. For reasons of clarity and space, we presented a small sample most frequent keyword requested. For better analysis, cumulative frequencies of confused abstracts are presented in TABLE III.

TABLE III. CUMULATIVE FREQUENCIES OF USER KEYWORDS IN ABSTRACTS OF IC

User keyw	Freq	User keyw	Fre	User keyw	Freq
Value	**1768**	**qualitative**	**144**	Sheet	46
industry	**632**	Risk	140	Score	42
market	**567**	**industrial**	**126**	Danish	36
empirical	556	**quantitative**	**115**	skandia	22
measurement	550	guidelines	114	cement	4
method	462	Wealth	104	**VAIC**	**0**
accounting	356	scorecard	70	**NICI**	**0**
Added	254	balanced	54	**IC-dVal**	**0**
qualitative	**144**	...	...	**WWTK**	**0**

The most frequent words are **market** and **value**. It is explained by the relationship between IC and the market value in certain methods of IC measurement (IC value = Market value - book value). It represents generally 4 or 5 times the book value (value of business given by accountants), which explains the existence of a very important intrinsic value that is *intellectual capital* in the form of the know-how of the experts in business. The words **industry** and **industrial** are very frequent; this implies that IC is measured also within industrial businesses. The **qualitative** word is better ranked than **quantitative** one because of the qualitative nature of IC which is difficult to quantify. The managers and accountants look for a credible tool to measure it. **VAIC**, **NICI**, **IC-dVal** and **WWTK** are user requested measurement methods of IC, but do not exist in the sample of articles containing "intellectual capital" in their titles.

2) Analysis of users' keywords in abstracts of KM area: The results of TABLE IV shows the cumulative frequencies of keywords in confused abstracts of KM.

TABLE IV: THE CUMULATIVE FREQUENCIES OF USERS' KEYWORDS IN KM

User keyw	Freq	User keyw	Freq	User keyw	Freq
Data	**782**	**potential**	**116**	Logic	22
performance	**772**	**intelligence**	**100**	Neural	12
sharing	**432**	**industrial**	**97**	Genetic	7
industry	**250**	Risk	93	Cement	**2**
practice	**229**	**communities**	**71**	commonKads	1
manufacturing	**171**	Fuzzy	67	datawarehouse	1
ontology	**157**	Database	60	**MSKM**	**0**
community	**136**	Center	35	**MASK**	**0**
Network	**133**	...	...	...	...

The word **data** is the densest, it expresses the close relationship between knowledge and data [15]; the data when it is processed becomes information and when it is used it becomes knowledge. The word **performance** reflects that knowledge contributes to improve performance of a company [16]. The word **sharing** expresses the sharing of knowledge, reinforces the collaboration between members of professional team and gives better results than the individual tasks. This collaboration is carried out by communities of practice (**community**, **communities**, **practice**); they are groups of employees using knowledge in their work. The industry is also present in the KM (**industry, manufacturing and industrial**). The word **intelligence** argues the relationship between **KM** and business intelligence. It is involved in enriching the knowledge base. **MSKM** and **MASK** are two methods of knowledge management but don't exist in the studied sample containing only articles with "knowledge management" in their titles.

3) Analysis of users' keywords in the full articles in KM: We used the PDF files of articles downloaded from SCOPUS. Fig. 1 shows the results when analyzing file by file. The red surrounded area represents the highest frequencies of users' keywords. It could be useful to a researcher looking for a specific topic by selecting only the articles with high frequencies of required keyword (topic) to use them in their literature review.

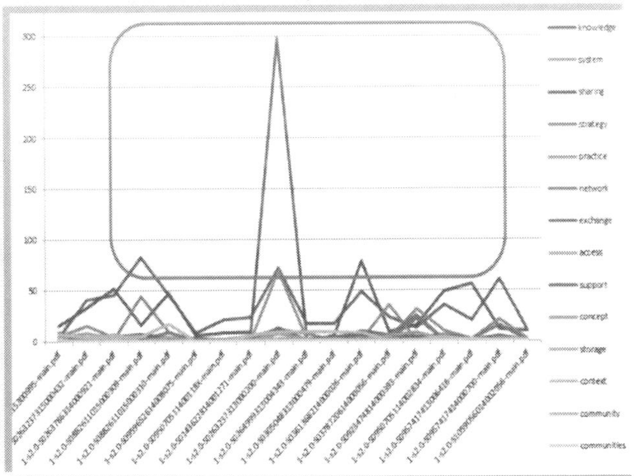

Figure 1. Frequencies of user keywords in PDF files individually in KM for 2015

In this individual analysis by PDF file, frequencies of keywords differ from one file to another. A global analysis would be more significant (TABLE V) when the researcher looks for the best area treating its topic (keyword) or to compare topics in the same area (IC, KM...etc).

TABLE V: GLOBAL USERS' KEYWORDS MEANS OF FREQUENCIES IN PDF KM IN 2015

User keyw	Freq	User keyw	Freq	User keyw	Freq
management	32,72	**Context**	**4,78**	Sharing	0,94
knowledge	39,94	**Network**	**3,94**	community	0,78
System	**8,5**	Support	3,94	Access	0,5
strategy	**5,94**	Concept	2,67	communities	0,39
practice	5,11	exchange	1,22	Storage	0,11

The word **system** is the most frequent; it relates to knowledge management systems. The word **context** refers to the contextual nature of knowledge and its extraction by data mining. **Network** refers to its important role in communication and collaboration to share knowledge by the communities of practice.

C. *Analysis of the densest words*

It is called density of words in the abstracts, the frequency of any word in a text corpus, not keywords provided by a user or by author. This analysis complements the previous one, because sometimes there are important new words discovered by this analysis but less known by the user. It is an automatic extraction of the densest words. Excel files containing only abstracts are used. In other words, it consists to find frequencies of words in a corpus filtered from stopwords which are in English (a, an, the, then, it, he, she, about, etc.), commonly conjunctions, pronouns or any other word not affecting the meaning of a text. The set of stopwords exists in the literature and it is taken into account in certain languages as R; the used language in this work.

1) Analysis of the densest words in the abstracts

a) Analysis of the densest words in the abstracts of IC: The means of the densest words in the IC area are calculated from 1995 to 2016. In all years, the word **intellectual** and **capital** have approximately the same appearance, the frequency of **capital** is more than **intellectual** (TABLE VI) because it exists other capitals: human capital, structural capital and organizational capital...etc.

TABLE VI: FREQUENCIES' MEANS OF DENSEST WORDS IN ABSTRACTS IC.

Dense word	Mean	Dense word	Mean	Dense word	Mean
Capital	**8549**	**managemen**	**1920**	findings	1057
intellectual	**6441**	**Value**	**1530**	information	906
Paper	**2181**	**companies**	**1282**	Can	893
Study	**2176**	**purpose**	**1199**	Limited	499
knowledge	**2067**	Firms	1120	creation	420
Research	**2007**	Model	1082	**indicators**	**376**
performance	**1933**	analysis	1065	implication	55

Paper, **study**, **research**, **findings** and **purpose** are generic words used in abstracts of any paper. **Indicators** express the different **values** of components of IC used by the measurement **models**.

b) Analysis of the densest words in the abstracts of KM: TABLE VII shows the averages of frequencies of densest words in KM area from 1997 to 2016. The generic words are same that IC ones. The word **process** indicates the knowledge management process optimization, which is subject to the reactivity of the knowledge system.

TABLE VII. MEAN OF THE DENSEST WORDS IN THE ABSTRACTS OF KM

Dense Word	Mean	Dense Word	Average	Dense Word	Mean
knowledge	1768,83	system	286,33	**innovation**	**156,50**
management	1053,42	paper	219,92	data	123,58
organisational	**268,83**	research	218,58	analysis	102,83
process	334,33	study	188,92	creation	86,33
information	300,33	devlopment	187,58	model	46,08

The word **organisational** is in third rank, it demonstrates the organizational aspect of knowledge management and the encouragement of organizational learning modules included in knowledge management systems. The word **innovation** is present as enrichment element of the knowledge system and the trigger of organisational learning.

2) Analysis of the densest words in articles' titles: The purpose of this analysis is very important, it is a decisive factor on the interest of a scientific article and its content.

a) Analysis of the densest words in the titles of the articles of IC: Fig. 2 shows the mean frequencies of the densest words in the titles of IC from 1998 to 2016.

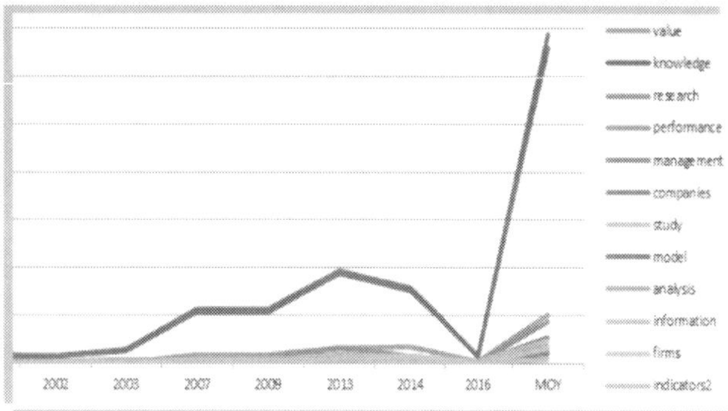

Figure 2. Densest words in the titles of IC, per year

It is noted that the two curves of the words **capital** and **intellectual** look the same on all the years since data is exported from SCOPUS have in their titles **intellectual capital**. The **capital** curve is slightly above the **intellectual** curve because there are other capitals. Their densities are highest in 2012 when the scientific production was highest for IC.

TABLE VIII. MEANS OF DENSEST WORDS IN IC TITLES

Dense word	Mean	Dense word	Mean	Dense word	Mean
capital	687	study	48	information	31
intellectual	659	value	35	model	22
performance	**101**	**analysis**	**34**	**research**	**19**
management	86	**companies**	**34**	**indicators**	**8**
knowledge	53	**firms**	**32**	...	...

The word **performance** is very dense (Table VIII), because IC improves business performance; it is expressed by the words **companies** and **firms**. This performance is measured by performance **indicator**.

b) Analysis of the densest words in the titles of KM articles: Fig. 3 shows the means frequencies of the dense words in titles of KM from 1997 to 2016.

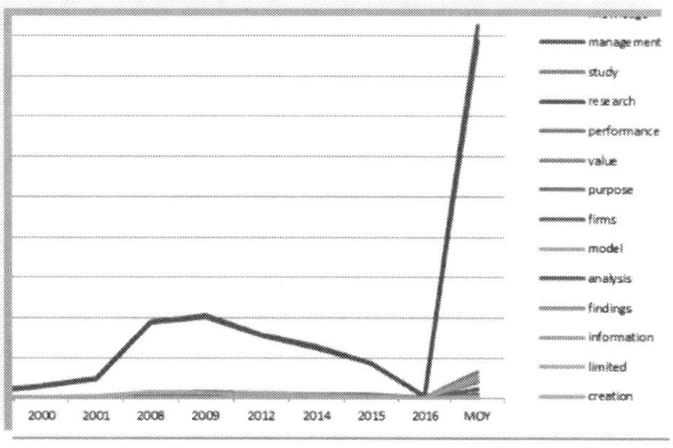

Figure 3. Densest words in titles of KM, per year

The two curves of **knowledge** and **management** look the same on all the years since data is exported from SCOPUS have in their titles knowledge management. The **knowledge** curve is slightly above the curve **management**, contrary to what was found in abstracts and PDF. There are other treatments of knowledge (knowledge acquisition, knowledge sharing…etc.). Their densities are highest in 2009 when scientific production was the highest for KM.

TABLE IX. MEANS OF THE DENSEST WORDS IN KM TITLES

Dense word	Mean	Dense word	Mean	Dense word	Mean
knowledge	4632	research	227	**creation**	**22**
management	4436	**performance**	**214**	findings	8
study	326	analysis	112	purpose	3
information	278	**firms**	**52**	limited	2
model	**240**	**value**	**36**	...	...

The word **model** expresses the models used for knowledge engineering, knowledge sharing, to improve **performance** of **firms** and assessment of **value** (Table IX).

3) Analysis of the densest words in the authors' keywords: The first analysis performed in Section A, concerns the author keyword as a whole expression, but this analysis seeks the densest words composing this keyword.

a) Analysis of the densest words in the authors' keywords of IC: Fig. 4 shows the frequencies' means of the densest words in the authors' keywords of IC from 1995 to 2016.

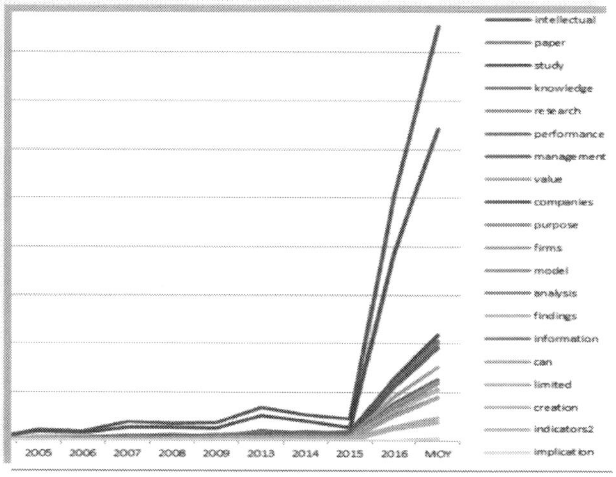

Figure 4. Densest words in authors' keywords of IC, per year

Over the years, the **intellectual** and **capital** curves have almost the same trends over time, but the **capital** one exceeds in density because there are other capitals than **intellectual**, such as financial capital and the components of intellectual capital.

TABLE X THE DENSEST WORDS IN THE AUTHORS' KEYWORDS OF IC

Dense word	Mean	Dense word	Mean	Dense word	Mean
Capital	450	management	101	findings	56
intellectual	339	**Value**	**81**	information	48
Paper	115	companies	67	Can	47
Study	115	purpose	63	Limited	26
knowledge	109	Firms	64	**creation**	**22**
research	106	**Model**	**57**	**Indicators**	**20**
performance	**102**	analysis	56	**implication**	**3**

The results of the density in the authors' keywords are similar to the density in titles, because in general the authors get their keywords from the title. Common dense words (Table X) are **performance**, **value**, **model**, **creation**, **indicator** and **involvement**.

b) Analysis of the densest words in the authors' keywords of KM: Fig. 5 shows the frequencies' means of the densest words in the authors' keywords of KM from 1998 to 2016.

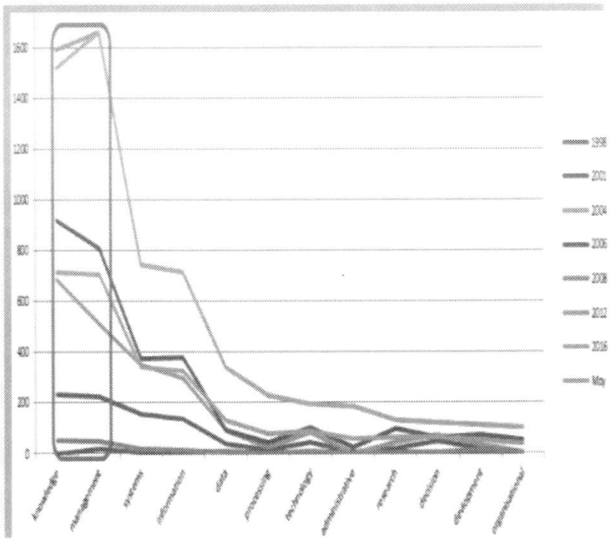

Figure 5. Densities of authors' keywords of KM, per year

In all years, the word **management** is less dense than the word **knowledge**, because there are other stages in KM process (e.g. knowledge transfer, knowledge capitalization…etc.).

TABLE XI DENSEST WORDS IN AUTHORS' KEYWORDS OF KM

Dense word	Avg	Dense word	Avg	Dense word	Avg
Knowledge	714	Data	131	Research	60
management	703	Technology	88	administrative	57
Systems	341	Processing	76	development	52
information	**323**	Decision	62	organisational	38

The results of the density in the authors' keywords are similar to the density in titles (TABLE XI), because in general the authors get their keywords from the title. Unlike IC, KM has no common dense words in the titles and authors' keywords at least in these first rows of TABLE XI except **information**, **knowledge** and **management**.

D. *Analysis of Zipf's law*

The analysis of Zipf's law is different from the densest words analysis seen in Section C. To apply Zipf's law, all words are taken into account, including the stopwords.

1) Analysis of Zipf's law in IC: A set of 655 among 1500 full articles in IC are used to create a corpus on which Zipf's law was applied. A set of 21365 different words appears in the corpus with different frequencies. The existing Zipf's law represents the found frequencies of words and the theoretic Zipf's law represents the theoretic frequency of word=Size of the corpus of text with stopwords (6911590 words) divided by the rank of the word after ordering by descending order of existing frequencies.

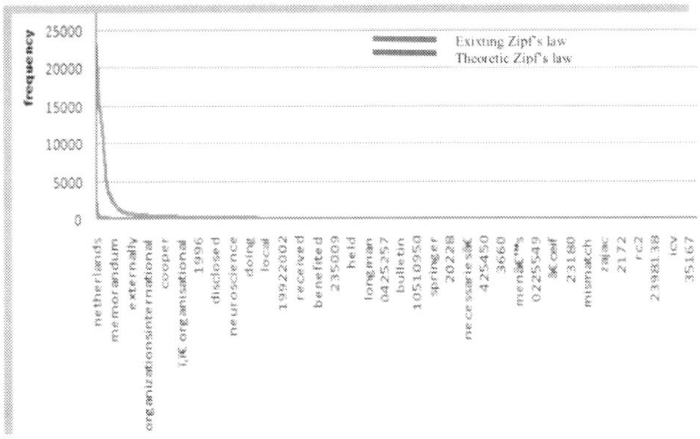

Figure 6. Zipf's law in IC corpus

Fig. 6 demonstrates that Zipf's law is globally verified and slightly different in the middle of curve.

2) Analysis of Zipf's law in KM: A set of 2420 among 10000 articles in KM are used to create a corpus on which we applied Zipf's law. A set of 18466 different words appears in the corpus with different frequencies. The theoretic Zipf's law represents the theoretic frequency of word=Size of the corpus of text with stopwords (6470344 words) divided by to the rank of the word after ordering by descending order of existing frequencies.

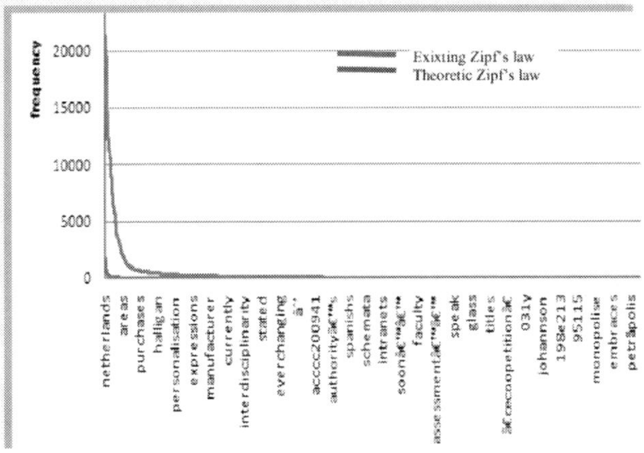

Figure 7. Zipf's law in KM corpus

Fig. 7 demonstrates that Zipf's law applied in KM is globally less verified than IC and slightly different in the middle of curve.

V. CONCLUSION

In this work, scientific articles (abstracts and full articles) were quantitatively analyzed to draw qualitative conclusions. These articles are related to the areas of intellectual capital and knowledge management. Each area was analyzed separately and it has been found different results especially for dense words. The densities are closely related to the scientific production of the area.

Keyword analysis allows the identification of existing levels of meaning in scientific articles as well as the unexpected trends in the area. Eight programs have been written in R language and applied to IC and KM. The goal is to delve into the exported data files from SCOPUS to collect the authors' keywords of scientific articles and calculate their frequencies. The full list of authors' keywords in both areas prepares the ground for the area glossary and ontology design. The goal was to find the frequencies of authors' keywords in the articles, keywords proposed by a user as needed and densest words in several items of articles (titles, abstracts, full files and authors' keywords). The latter is the most significant; it allows discovering new concepts introduced in the area for enrichment of glossaries and ontologies which could be proposed for a research area. KM and IC have many common concepts as management, performance, model, value.

Generally, Zipf's law is valid in IC and KM fields for the database SCOPUS. Despite the fact that the sample of full articles in KM is larger than IC ones, the corpus of IC is richer in keywords.

As perspectives, we could apply other sets of keywords indicators to draw other conclusions. This work prepares the ground for the creation of glossaries and ontologies for both IC and KM areas and it addresses the semantic relationships between keywords.

For the representation of frequency, one would think to develop a tool for representing words in clouds as the frequency and relevance criteria specified by the user.

For authors' keywords, an analysis by group of words is possible because there are synonyms which may offer a sum of frequencies and one can calculate the frequency of the group of words. This grouping step requires a thorough knowledge of words and their use in the search area, and if we would do it automatically, this would require an additional effort of semantic links expressed by other ontologies or semantic analysis tools. The extension can be the logical combinations between several keywords in the search query. At the end, the designed programs can be applied to any area of research exported from SCOPUS database. To use them for other databases, it will be necessary to slightly adapt them to the shape of input data.

References

[1] M. Karl Wiig, "Integrating intellectual capital and knowledge management", Long Range Planning, vol. 30, No. 3, pp. 399-405, 1997.

[2] I. J. Lopez-Veyna, J. V. Sosa-Sosa and I. Lopez-Arevalo, "A low redundancy strategy for keyword search in structured and semi-structured data Information Sciences", Information Sciences, vol. 288, pp. 135-152, 2014.

[3] C. C. Bang, Information systems frontiers: Keyword analysis and classification, Information Systems Frontiers, vol. 17, No. 1, pp. 217-237, 2015.

[4] C. Jaewoo and K. Woonsun, "Themes and trends in Korean educational technology research: A social network analysis of keywords", Procedia - Social and Behavioral Sciences, vol. 131, pp. 171 – 176, 2014.

[5] W. Bihu, X. Honggen, D. Xiaoli, W. Mu and X. Lan, "Tourism knowledge domains: A Keyword Analysis", Asia Pacific Journal of Tourism Research, vol. 17, No. 4, pp. 355-380, 2012.

[6] G. F. Khan and J. Wood, "Information technology management domain: emerging themes and keyword analysis", Scientometrics, 105: 959. doi:10.1007/s11192-015-1712-5, 2015.

[7] A. Andrés, Measuring academic research: How to undertake a bibliometric study, Chandos Publishing, 2009.

[8] W. Li, "Random Texts Exhibit Zipfs-Law-Like Word Frequency Distribution", IEEE Transactions on information theory, vol. 38, No. 6 pp. 1842-1845, 1992.

[9] L. A. Adamic and B. A. Huberman, "Zipf's law and the Internet", Glottometrics, vol. 3, pp.143-150, 2002.

[14] M. Habibi and A. Popescu-Belis, "Diverse keyword Extraction from Conversations", The fifty first Annual Meeting of the Association for Computational Linguistics, pp. 651-657, 2013.

[15] D. Trieschnigg, D. Nguyen and M. Theune, "Learning to Extract Folktale Keywords", University of Twente, pp 1-9, 2013.

[16] L. Marujo et al, Automatic Keyword extraction on Twitter, University of Carnegie Mellon, 2014.

[17] S. Klapdor, M. Anderl, F. Wangenheim and J. H. Schuman, "Finding the right words: the influence of keyword characteristics on performance of paid search campaigns", Journal of Interactive Marketing, vol. 28, pp. 285–301, 2014.

[18] R. Rizzo, M. José and M. Pérez, "A key perspective on specialized lexis: keywords in telecommunication engineering for CLIL", Procedia - Social and Behavioral Sciences, vol. 198, pp. 386 – 396, 2015.

[19] A. Onan, S. Korukoglu and H. Bulut, "Ensemble of keyword extraction methods and classifiers in text classification", Expert systems with applications, vol. 57, pp. 232-247, 2016.

[20] I. Tuomi, "Data is more than knowledge: Implications of the reversed knowledge hierarchy for knowledge management and organizational memory", Journal of Management Information Systems, vol. 16, No. 3, pp 103-117, 1999.

[21] S. Aitouche, M. D. Mouss, A. Kaanit, K. Bouhafna, W. Mammeri and A. Chabbi, "SKACICM a method for development of knowledge management and innovation system e-KnowSphere", International journal of Knowledge and Web Intelligence (IJKWI), vol. 5, No. 2, pp. 105-126, 2015.

[22] S. Aitouche et al, "A hybrid method to develop a knowledge management system", The Sixth International Conference on Information, Process, and Knowledge Management (EKNOW 2014), IARIA, pp. 77-83, Mar 2014, ISSN: 2308-4375 ISBN: 978-1-61208-329-2,

[23] M. Titah, M.D. Mouss, S. Aitouche, "An implementation tool for the expertise model using CommonKADS methodology", The Sixth International Conference on Information, Process, and Knowledge Management (EKNOW 2014), IARIA, pp. 70-76, Mar 2014,ISSN:2308-4375, ISBN: 978-1-61208-329-2.

[24] H. Barki, S. Rivard and J. Talbot, "An information systems keyword classification scheme", MIS Quarterly, vol. 12, No. 2, pp. 299-322, 1988.

On How Networks Stabilize User Interest Based Methods and Vice Versa

László Grad-Gyenge
University Eötvös Loránd
Budapest, Hungary
laszlo.grad-gyenge@inf.elte.hu

Peter Filzmoser
TU Vienna
Vienna, Austria
peter.filzmoser@tuwien.ac.at

Abstract—**This paper presents the evaluation of two graph-based recommendation methods compared to collaborative filtering as the baseline. The evaluation is primarily based on the investigation of the Average Receiver operating Characteristic curve on the MovieLens dataset. The presented methods operate on the knowledge graph, which information representation technique is also discussed in this paper. The evaluation results show that combining a network based and a user interest based method leads to a more stable performance and an increase in the recommendation quality.**

***Keywords*–recommender system; graph based; knowledge graph; explicit feedback; receiver operating characteristic**

I. Introduction

Collaborative filtering and content-based filtering are two prominent classes of the recommender systems. The essence of collaborative filtering is that the recommendations are derived only from user-item interactions. Content-based techniques primarily focus on item attributes. Thinking in general, utilizing the user attributes can also be treated as a content-based technique. Our work is based on a graph based information representation technique, which is capable to represent user-item interactions, item attributes and user attributes at the same abstraction level. We call this representation technique the knowledge graph. This technique can be treated as a hybridization method at the information representation level.

Graph based recommender systems provide an alternative aspect to the widely used, matrix or tensor oriented methods. An advantage of the graph based representation is the potential to develop recommendation methods operating on networks. Referring to the results of network science, utilizing networks, the calculation methods can be improved regarding to their robustness and stability. In addition, the graph based representation has the capability to represent heterogeneous information sources and to provide a general information representation method. Working with heterogeneous information can be helpful to eliminate the cold start problem, as the more information is available, the higher is the chance to connect the current user to the items in the graph.

In our work, we focus on separating the information representation method from the calculation methods. We do this in order to have a clearer methodological approach. As the representation method provides the hybridization technique, two calculation methods, spreading activation and recommendation spreading is described and compared to the performance of collaborative filtering. Recommendation spreading basically alloys spreading activation and collaborative filtering. As recommendation spreading does not use any representation technique to compress the adjacency matrix of the graph, we compare the performance of recommendation spreading to the performance of collaborative filtering.

Grad-Gyenge et al. [1] evaluate recommendation spreading and collaborative filtering regarding to the mean absolute error (MAE) and the coverage of the mentioned methods. As list based recommendations are more in the focus of interest of the research on recommendation techniques, a Receiver operating Characteristic (RoC) based evaluation of the methods is presented. In order to adapt the RoC measure to the field of recommender systems, the Average Receiver operating Characteristic (ARoC) evaluation method is introduced. Providing an overview of the performance of the evaluated method, ARoC interprets the RoC in the case of recommender systems, as the RoC graphs are averaged over all users in the knowledge graph. The result is a more robust measure and a smoother graph. An additional advantage of the evaluation method is that it also provides information about the completeness of the list of retrieved items.

The contribution of the paper can be summarized as follows. The evaluation results show that regarding to the ARoC, recommendation spreading is capable to incorporate the advantages of spreading activation and collaborative filtering, thus we show that the information found in the network can stabilize rating value based methods and also vice versa. The information found in rating values can improve the network based calculation. We also show that in the information sparse case, the rating estimation based methods show better performance than ranking based methods.

Section II presents related research conducted. Section III discusses the graph based information representation technique. Section IV describes the recommendation methods evaluated in the paper. Section V introduces ARoC, the evaluation method. Section VI presents the results of the evaluation. Section VII concludes the paper and gives insight into our plans for the future.

II. Related Work

To discuss related research conducted, we focus on graph based information representation techniques, spreading activation based methods and RoC evaluation methods. Regarding to graph based information representation and spreading activation based techniques, the improvement presented in this paper can be found in the performance of recommendation spreading.

Although not widely used, the graph based information representation technique presents in the field of recommender systems. State of the art research is also conducted on graph based representation. Tiroshi et al. [2] involve graph representation to work with social data. Lee et al. [3] represents correlations between the entities in a graph. Similarly to the representation presented in this paper, Lee at al. [4] represents content-based and collaborative filtering information in a heterogeneous graph.

Next to ontology representation, graphs are typically involved to model the social relationships. To mention asymmetric networks, Ziegler et al. [5], Guha et al. [6], Jsang et al. [7], Massa et al. [8] calculate the recommendations with the help of the trust network. Symmetric networks are also involved, as He et al. [9], Konstas et al. [10] and Guy et al. [11] calculate recommendations with the help of the social network. Layered graphs, as less generalized approaches also can be found in the literature. Cantador et al. [12] apply a clustering technique on a multi-layered graph. Kazienko et al. [13] calculate recommendations on a layered graph.

Representing heterogeneous information in the knowledge graph is also in the focus of intense research. Burke et al. [14] define a heterogeneous network in order to be able to model various recommendation cases as user-based k-Nearest Neighbors algorithm (k-NN) with the user-tag matrix, user-based k-NN with the user-resource matrix, item-based k-NN with the resource-tag matrix and item-based k-NN with the resource-user matrix. Yu et al. [15] introduce the PathSim measure to compare paths in the knowledge graph to measure the similarity between the observed and the potential paths. Catherine et al. [16] derive recommendations with a probabilistic logic approach on the knowledge graph. Hu et al. [17] present label propagation for lead generation. Kouki et al. [18] define a probabilistic framework as a hybridization technique.

Spreading activation is widely used in different domains to derive recommendations. Alvarez et al. define ONTO-SPREAD, a well-elaborated, spreading activation based method for medical systems [19]. Troussov et al. present the investigation of different decay configurations of spreading activation in a tag aware recommendation scenario [20]. Gao et al. argue that the domain knowledge and user interests on items are to be represented in the same ontology [21]. Blanco-Fernandez et al. utilize spreading activation to conduct content based reasoning [22]. In their work, they model the semantics of the preferences of the users. They stress out that spreading activation is a potential method to avoid overspecialisation. Jiang et al. utilize spreading activation to calculate recommendations on an ontology based user model [23]. The primary goal of Hussein et al. is to close the gap between context-awareness and self-adaptation [24]. To perform this task, SPREADR, a spreading activation based recommendation method is defined. Codina et al. present a semantic recommendation method to estimate user ratings on items with a reasoning technique [25]. In their work, the item score is defined as the weighted average of the related concepts.

Herlocker et al. describe a method to prepare the RoC curve [26], which is a known evaluation technique in the field of recommender systems. They leave the definition of the relevance of an item for the specific user open, thus the relevance is to be defined for the actual evaluation case. For example, in the case of rating estimation methods, the relevance can be defined based on a threshold value. To draw an RoC graph, the curve is started from the origin and an iteration is conducted on the recommendation result list. For each item, the relevance is determined. If the item is relevant, then the curve is drawn one step vertically. If the item is not relevant, then the curve is drawn one step horizontally. Herlocker et al. define the RoC curve for the specified user. As typically there are several users utilizing a recommender system, a possible enhancement of the RoC should examine the performance of the recommendation method regarding to all users or a well defined subset of users.

Cremonesi et al. also utilize the RoC curve to evaluate their recommendation methods [27]. In their work, Cremonesi et al. define two variants of the RoC curve and denote them as ROC1 and ROC2. ROC1 uses a threshold based technique to identify true positives, false positives, true negatives and false negatives. ROC2 is suitable for ranked lists and is defined for both the binary and the non-binary case. An important aspect of their work is that Cremonesi et al. use a user sampling technique. To focus on users with relatively sparse on item preferences, they evaluate their methods on the subset of users containing users issued at most 99 ratings.

Improvements to the RoC curve can also be found in the literature. Schein et al. introduce CROC, the Customer RoC curve [28]. In their work, Schein et al. stress out the divergence in the lengths of the recommendation lists of different users. To solve this problem, they propose a technique to unify the lengths of the recommendation lists and calculate the measures necessary to produce the RoC curve based on the unified lists. Also mentioning the problem of different lengths of item lists, Schröder et al. focuses on the first n items of the recommendation lists [29].

III. Representation Technique

The advantage of the graph based knowledge base is the capability to represent heterogeneous information sources in the same structure. In this section, a modelling technique is discussed, which is capable to store the information necessary for both collaborative and content-based filtering. In special cases, this technique can also act as the background of rule based systems. A similar representation technique is used by Lee et al. [4], Burke et al. [14], Yu et al. [15], Kouki et al. [18] and Grad-Gyenge et al. [1].

This section presents the definition of the information representation method and also provides theoretical insights. In order to clarify the approach, the concrete dataset and its representation is described in this section.

A. Definition

The information is represented in a labelled multigraph. We refer to it as the knowledge graph or the knowledge base and define it in Equation (1).

$$\mathcal{K} = (N, E, T_N, T_E, t_N, t_E, r), \tag{1}$$

where N represents the set of nodes in the graph, $E \subseteq \{\{u, v\} | u \in N \wedge v \in N \wedge u \neq v\}$ represents the set of undirected edges between the nodes. T_N denotes the set of node types and T_E denotes the set of edge types. The function $t_N \subset N \times T_N$ assigns a node type to each node, the function $t_E \subset E \times T_E$ assigns an edge type to each edge. The partial function $r \subset E \times \mathbb{R}$ assigns a rating value to specific edges. The function is partial, as in most cases not all the edges

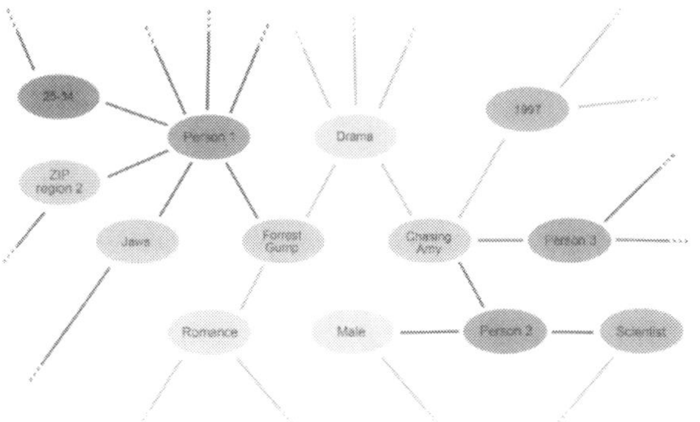

Figure 1. A detailed view of the MovieLens dataset represented in the knowledge graph.

represent a rating. Although it is formally not defined, in the implementation, due to performance reasons, we avoid parallel edges of the same type between the same pair of nodes. We would also like to mention here that type assignments do not influence the final recommendation result and are introduced for completeness.

B. MovieLens

The numerical experiment is conducted on the MovieLens dataset [30]. Analysing the available MovieLens versions, we decided to use the MovieLens 1M dataset, as in addition to containing true rating values, this dataset is also rich in user and item attributes. The user attributes are gender, age category, occupation and ZIP code. The item attributes are year of release and list of genres.

As illustrated in Fig. 1, the user and item attributes are modelled in the knowledge graph similarly how semantic networks represent the information. Light blue nodes as `Jaws`, `Forrest Gump` and `Chasing Amy` represent the items (movies). Lilac nodes as `Person 1`, `Person2` and `Person3` represent the persons. Drab nodes as `Romance` and `Drama` represent the genres. The gray node represents the gender `Male`. The blue node represents the occupation `Scientist`. The light brown node represents the release year `1997`. The green node represents the `ZIP region 2`. The red node represents the age category `25-34`.

Each user is represented with a node of type `Person`. A node type is introduced to represent each kind of user attributes. To represent the user attributes, a node of the appropriate type is created for each attribute value. Nodes of type `Gender` represent the genders. Nodes of type `AgeCategory` represent the age categories. Nodes of type `Occupation` represent the occupations. Nodes of type `ZipCodeRegion` represent the zip code regions. In this case the first digit of the zip code is used as it determines the U.S. region. To model that a user has a specific attribute value, the node representing the user is connected to the node representing the attribute value with an edge of the appropriate type. To model this information, edge types `PersonGender`, `PersonAgeCategory`, `PersonOccupation` and `PersonZipCodeRegion` are introduced, respectively.

Each item is represented with a node of type `Item`. To represent the item attributes, a node of the appropriate type is created for each attribute value. Nodes of type `Genre` represent the genres. An item can have multiple genres. In this case, the item node is connected to multiple genre nodes. Nodes of type `YearOfRelease` represent the years of release. To model that an item has a specific attribute value, the node representing the item is connected to the node representing the attribute value with an edge of the appropriate type. To model this information, edge types `PersonGender`, `PersonAgeCategory`, `PersonOccupation` and `PersonZipCodeRegion` are introduced, respectively.

The MovieLens 1M dataset contains 1 000 209 true ratings. Each true rating consists of an item, an user, a rating value and a time-stamp the rating event has been recorded at. The rating values are integer numbers and are in the interval $[1, 5]$. In our experiment, the rating values are normalized and are transformed linearly into the interval $[0.2, 1]$ by a division by 5. We denote the set of known true rating events with T and an element of the set with t. To access the attributes of true rating t, $t.u$, $t.i$, $t.v$ and $t.t$ stands for the user, item, value and time-stamp of rating t, respectively.

In the case a rating is added to the knowledge base, a new edge of type `ItemRating` is created between the node representing the user and the node representing the rated item. The rating value is assigned to the edge using the function r.

C. The Limes of the Hybridization

To present the amount of information the methods operate on in this experiment, Table I summarizes the count of nodes and edges in the knowledge graph. Subtable Ia contains the number of nodes of each node type. Subtable Ib presents the number of edges of each edge type. The total number of nodes is 10 062. The total number of edges not counting edges of type `ItemRating` is 34 451.

TABLE I. COUNT OF NODE AND EDGE TYPES IN THE MOVIELENS DATASET.

(a) Count of node types.

Node type	Count
Person	6 040
AgeCategory	7
Gender	2
Occupation	21
ZipCodeRegion	10
Item	3 883
Genre	18
YearOfRelease	81

(b) Count of edge types.

Edge type	Count
PersonAgeCategory	6 040
PersonGender	6 040
PersonOccupation	6 040
PersonZipCodeRegion	6 040
ItemGenre	6 408
ItemYearOfRelease	3 883
ItemRating	1 000 209

The representation technique models the information necessary to conduct both collaborative and content-based filtering methods. A properly defined calculation method should treat these information sources as general. It means that deriving recommendations, the calculation method should process the edges of different type at the same algorithmic abstraction level.

In the cold start case, when the knowledge base is sparse on `ItemRating` edges and is relatively dense on edges representing content-based information, the recommendation method can be treated as content-based. Thinking about the magnitude of the number of edges of type `ItemRating` (1 000 209) and other, content-based edges (34 451), as during the operation, the knowledge base is filled with user interaction, the recommendations are to be become more collaborative. In other words, the hybridization technique inherently ensures content-based recommendations in the cold start case and inherently transforms the methods operating on the top of it to be collaborative as it is populated with edges representing user-item interaction.

IV. Recommendation Methods

In our experiment, collaborative filtering, spreading activation, recommendation spreading and random recommendations are evaluated. The methods are defined in the following subsections.

A. Collaborative Filtering

We utilize a representation technique, which gives a different aspect to the more or less traditional, matrix based methods. Another problem of the matrix based representation is the restricted ability to represent heterogeneous information sources. A well researched direction to solve this issue is to involve tensors and to conduct tensor factorization [31].

Collaborative filtering [30] calculates rating estimations basically by averaging the known ratings on the item in question. The weight of a rating is the similarity of the user issuing the rating to the user the recommendations are generated for. To be more exact, instead of aggregating the known ratings, the differences from the mean ratings are averaged and then addded to the mean rating of the user. The rating estimation formula for user u on item i on our knowledge base is defined in Equation (2).

$$\hat{r}_{u,i} = \bar{r}_u + \frac{\sum_{e \in E_r, \{v,i\}=e, v \neq i, u \neq v} (r(e) - \bar{r_v}) s_{u,v}}{\sum_{e \in E_r, \{v,i\}=e, v \neq i, u \neq v} s_{u,v}}, \quad (2)$$

where $\hat{r}_{u,i}$ denotes the estimated rating value for user u on item i. The average of the known ratings is denoted by $\bar{r}_u$. To calculate the similarity between u and v, the Pearson correlation formula is utilized on the rating values of the common rated items.

B. Spreading Activation

Spreading activation [32] is widely used on ontologies, semantic networks, associative networks and RDF knowledge bases [33]. To utilize the method on the knowledge graph, spreading activation is used to calculate ranking values for the items. In this case no rating estimation is calculated.

Spreading activation is an iterative method with a `step limit` (c) based termination criteria. To generate item rankings, the method maintains the activation of the nodes. The function $a_{(i)} \subset N \times \mathbf{R}$ assigns an activation value to each node in the graph in each iteration step. In the initial step the activation of the nodes is set to 0 except for n_s, as $a_{(0)}(n_s) = 1$. The notation n_s stands for the source node, the node representing the user.

During the iteration, the activation of the nodes is propagated in the network. In each step, (i) a part of the activation of the nodes is distributed to the neighbour nodes equally and (ii) the activation of the nodes is relaxed. The parameter `spreading relax` (r_s) controls the amount of activation to distribute. The parameter `activation relax` (r_a) determines the ratio the activation of the nodes are to be relaxed. The update of the activation is conducted according to the rule defined in Equation (3).

$$a_{(i+1)}(n) = r_a a_{(i)}(n) + r_s \sum_{m \in M_n} \frac{a_{(i)}(m)}{|M_n|}, \quad (3)$$

where $n \in N$, $i \geq 0$. The set containing the neighbour nodes of n is denoted with M_n, as $M_n = \{m | \{m, n\} \in E\}$.

The iteration is performed until the `step limit` (c) is reached. The rank of each node is defined as its activation after the iteration has been stopped.

C. Recommendation Spreading

Recommendation spreading introduced by Grad-Gyenge et al. can be treated as the generalization of collaborative filtering for the graph based knowledge base [1]. The method is based on spreading activation but focuses on rating estimation. As already discussed, collaborative filtering defines a weighted average of the known rating values. In the case of collaborative filtering, the weights are determined by the similarity of the users. In the case of recommendation spreading, a distance like measure is defined between the user to generate the recommendations for and the edges representing the known rating values. To calculate the distance, an iteration is conducted with a `step limit` (c) based termination criteria. The activations are calculated using the same formula as in the case of the spreading activation. In each iteration step, the amount of flown through activation is summarized for the edges, as defined in Equation (4).

$$A_e = \sum_{i \in [0, s-1], m \in e, t_N(m) = Person} r_s \frac{a_{(i)}(m)}{|M_n|}, \quad (4)$$

where $e \in E$. The set containing the neighbour nodes of n is denoted with M_n, as $M_n = \{m | \{m, n\} \in E\}$.

To estimate the rating of an item, recommendation spreading calculates a weighted average. The weight of a rating is the flown through activation in the spreading iteration, as defined in Equation (5).

$$\hat{r}_{u,i} = \bar{r}_u + \frac{\sum_{e \in E_r, \{v,i\}=e, v \neq i, u \neq v} (r(e) - \bar{r_v}) A_e}{\sum_{e \in E_r, \{v,i\}=e, v \neq i, u \neq v} A_e}. \quad (5)$$

D. The Random Method

The random method is involved in the experiment for the following reasons. Thinking about the no free lunch theorem [34], the method can act as the theoretical baseline for all the methods. The other reason to involve random recommendations into the experiment is to control the mathematical correctness of our evaluation measure. A more or less trivial consequence of the definition of the RoC curve is that the performance of random recommendations should show a minor diagonal on the RoC graph.

E. List Recommendations

Collaborative filtering and recommendation spreading calculates a rating estimation for each item. Based on the rating estimation of the items, the list of recommended items is assembled by sorting the items in descending order by their rating estimation. As spreading activation calculates a ranking value for each item, the list of recommended items in this case is assembled by sorting the items in descending order by their rank.

We introduce function m as the notation for calculating the list of the recommended items for user u using method m over knowledge base $\mathcal{K}$, as defined in Equation (6).

$$m_{\mathcal{K}}(u). \tag{6}$$

V. Evaluation Method

The evaluation of the recommendation methods is conducted with ARoC, a RoC based evaluation technique, which is to be defined in this section. An important parameter of the evaluation method is the amount of rating edges to be inserted in the knowledge base in addition to the content-based information.

A. Initial Information

The evaluation of the recommendation techniques analysed in this paper is strongly connected to the information content contained in the knowledge base. Each evaluation starts with a knowledge graph containing only the user and the item attribute edges. In this case, there is no user preference stored in the knowledge graph. To incorporate also user preference information, a specified number of ratings is added to the knowledge base by creating edges of type `ItemRating`. As our intention is to model real-world applications, in this case, the first n ratings are selected from the true ratings in ascending order by their time-stamp. The first n ratings are called training set and are denoted with T_i.

B. Definitions

The evaluation of the methods is based on the RoC curve. Its essence is to plot the true positive rate (TPR) of the method in question against its false positive rate (FPR) on a single plot. RoC is typically used in the case of binary classification. In our experiment an item is defined to be positive for a particular user if the training data contains a true rating value higher than a pre-defined threshold. An item is defined to be negative if the value of the true rating is lower than the threshold. To formalize it, the predicate p stands for the positive case and the predicate n stands for the negative case as defined in Equations (7) and (8), respectively.

$$p_\Theta(u,i) = \exists t \in T : u = t.u \wedge i = t.i \wedge t.v \geq \Theta, \tag{7}$$

$$n_\Theta(u,i) = \exists t \in T : u = t.u \wedge i = t.i \wedge t.v < \Theta. \tag{8}$$

Based on the predicates, the true positive and related measures are to be defined. The functions TP, FP, TN, FN calculate the number of true positive, false positive, true negative and false negative items, respectively. The functions are defined in Equations (9), (10), (11) and (12), recpectively.

$$TP_{\Theta,k}(u,l) = |\{i \in I \mid p_\Theta(u,i) \wedge \exists j \leq k : i = l_j\}|, \tag{9}$$

$$FP_{\Theta,k}(u,l) = |\{i \in I \mid n_\Theta(u,i) \wedge \exists j \leq k : i = l_j\}|, \tag{10}$$

$$TN_{\Theta,k}(u,l) = |\{i \in I \mid n_\Theta(u,i) \wedge \nexists j \leq k : i = l_j\}|, \tag{11}$$

$$FN_{\Theta,k}(u,l) = |\{i \in I \mid p_\Theta(u,i) \wedge \nexists j \leq k : i = l_j\}|. \tag{12}$$

Functions TP, FP, TN and FN count the items for user u on the list of items l. The function attribute Θ specifies the threshold value. The function attribute k specifies the length the item list should be analized for.

The RoC curve is produced by plotting the TPR against the FPR in a graph. The TPR is the ratio of positive items retrieved compared to all the positive items. The FPR is the ratio of negative items retrieved compared to all the negative items. The functions are defined in Equations (13) and (14), recpectively.

$$TPR_{\Theta,k}(u,l) = \frac{TP_{\Theta,k}(u,l)}{TP_{\Theta,k}(u,l) + FN_{\Theta,k}(u,l)}, \tag{13}$$

$$FPR_{\Theta,k}(u,l) = \frac{FP_{\Theta,k}(u,l)}{FP_{\Theta,k}(u,l) + TN_{\Theta,k}(u,l)}. \tag{14}$$

The function TPR and FPR deliver the appropriate ratio values for user u on the list of items l. The function attribute Θ specifies the threshold value. The function attribute k specifies the length the item list should be analized for.

The functions TPR and FPR are to be calculated for a given user and list of items. In order to be able to plot the RoC curve, a distinguished user has to be selected from the knowledge base. As this selection procedure is not a straightforward task, instead of calculating TPR and FPR for a specific user, the average of these measures is calculated for all the users in the dataset. For each user, the list of items is delivered by the evaluated recommendation method, thus l is to be substituted to $m_{\mathcal{K}}(u)$ as presented in Equations (15) and (16).

$$ATPR_{\Theta,k}(m) = \frac{\sum_{u \in U} TPR_{\Theta,k}(u, m_{\mathcal{K}}(u))}{|U|}, \tag{15}$$

$$AFPR_{\Theta,k}(m) = \frac{\sum_{u \in U} FPR_{\Theta,k}(u, m_{\mathcal{K}}(u))}{|U|}, \tag{16}$$

where m denotes the evaluated method. The method operates on the knowledge base $\mathcal{K}$. The set U denotes the set of users ($U = \{u \in N \mid t_N(u) = Person\}$).

C. ARoC

Having the underlying measures defined, an RoC based evaluation method is to be introduced, the Average Receiver operating Characteristic, the ARoC. The definition of the ARoC is based on $ATPR$ and $AFPR$. To draw the RoC curve of method m, k is iterated from zero to the length of the longest list of recommended items. For each value of k, a mark is plotted onto the graph. The coordinates of the mark are calculated as the value of $ATPR_{\Theta,k}(m)$ and $AFPR_{\Theta,k}(m)$.

As its name indicates, ARoC averages the RoC graphs over all the users into a single graph. Thanks to the aggregation, ARoC provides a more robust measure and also a smoother graph. The difference between RoC and ARoC can also be found in the drawing method. While the drawing of the RoC curve is based on vertical and horizontal steps of the same unit, the coordinates of the ARoC graph is defined by the $ATPR$ and $AFPR$ function. This is also the reason why the ARoC graph is not necessarily a continuous curve.

The $ATPR_{\Theta,k}$ and the $AFPR_{\Theta,k}$ measures are calculated as the averages on the lists of recommended items for the specified list length k. As mentioned in Section II, the recommendation lists typically differ in their length, as the reachable item nodes differ for each user. This is the reason why the higher is value of k, the lower is the amount of the averaged TPR and FPR measures.

Unlike random item selection, most recommendation methods do not retrieve the whole set of recommendable items. To illustrate this phenomenon in the graph oriented aspect, it is not ensured that all the items are linked to the users with the appropriate path. Looking at the ARoC graphs presented in Section VI, especially in the case of collaborative filtering and recommendation spreading, the graph of the methods do not reach the upper-right corner because of the aforementioned reason. We think about this property of the ARoC method as a useful feature, as next to illustrating the TPR and FPR of the methods, it also provides information about the completeness of the retrieved items.

VI. Evaluation Results

The methods described in Section IV are evaluated on the MovieLens dataset represented in the knowledge graph defined in Section III. The evaluation is based on the ARoC curve as defined in Section V.

To evaluate the methods, various the following parameter settings of Θ are evaluated 0.4, 0.6, 0.8 and 1.0. Due to space limitations, the 0.8 case is presented. This is also the most representative case. To interpret the 0.8 value, items with rating 4 or 5 are treated positive. Table II contains the presented method configurations. Column `Name` contains the short name of the method. Column `Method` holds the type of the method. Column `Configuration` defines the configuration parameters of the methods if there is any. Our past results [1] show that the examined methods are not sensitive to the different r_a and r_s settings. These results are not presented in this paper due to space limitations. Regarding to the setting of c, those configurations are presented, which at most represent the evaluation properties of the specific method.

A. ARoC

As we are interested in how the amount of rating edges in the knowledge base influences the performance of the methods, the evaluation is organized into 4 scenarios. The scenarios differ in the size of the training set (T_i). To refer to it later, the `10k`, `20k`, `40k` and `200k` shorthands are introduced for the case with 10 000, 20 000, 40 000 and 200 000 rating values, respectively. Fig. 2 contains the ARoC graph of the discussed methods with different $|T_i|$ settings in its subfigures.

TABLE II. Method configurations

Name	Method	Configuration
CF	Collaborative Filtering	–
SA	Spreading Activation	$c = 5, r_a = 0.5, r_s = 0.5$
RS	Recommendation Spreading	$c = 5, r_a = 0.5, r_s = 0.5$
RND	Random Method	–

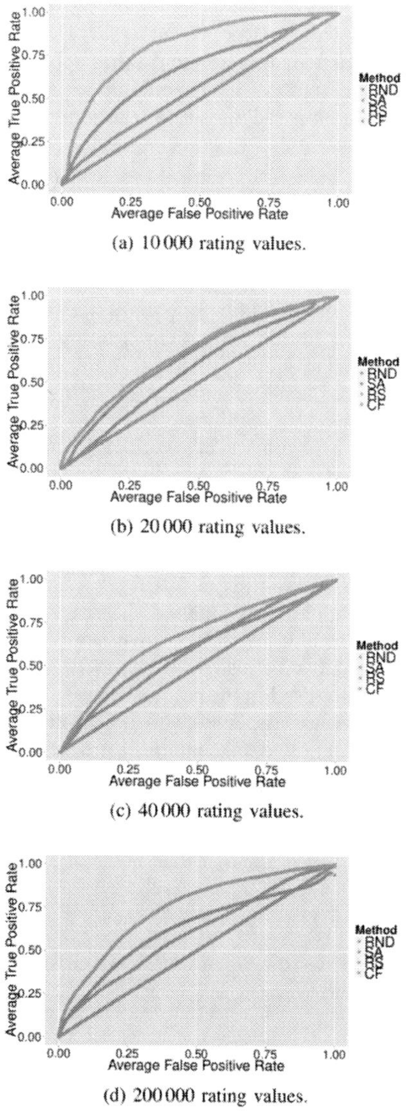

(a) 10 000 rating values.

(b) 20 000 rating values.

(c) 40 000 rating values.

(d) 200 000 rating values.

Figure 2. The ARoC curve of the evaluated methods on the knowledge containing different number of rating values.

The primary result of the evaluation is that RS outperforms the other methods in all the 4 scenarios. The advantage of the method stands out more in the information sparse (`10k`) and in the information dense (`200k`) cases.

Comparing the CF and the SA, the performane of the methods vary with the different amount of rating values in the knowledge graph. While in the `10k` scenario, the CF is dominant, in the `20k` case, the SA performs better. In the `40k` and the `200k` case, the CF performs better on the lower domain of k than SA then the graph of the CF and the SA are crossing each other. In these cases, the performance of the methods is ambigously comparable.

Analysing the performance of the CF on high k values, Fig. 2d shows that the performance of the CF falls below the performance of the RND. Referring to the no free lunch theorem [34], this is an important theoretical result. In addition, the curve of the CF is not monotonic and is also not continous. We explain it as follows. The ARoC measure is defined to show the average performance of the precision and recall measures over all users of the dataset. As the length of the recommendation lists grows, the amount of the averaged measures decreases causing non-monotonicity.

As mentioned in Section V-C, an important feature of the ARoC curve is that the coverage of the evaluated methods can be read from its graph. For example, the curve of CF on Fig. 2a does not reach the upper-right corner meaning that the CF retrieves only a subset of relevant items for the users. Analysing the methods from this aspect, it can be seen that the SA has the highest coverage, the RS is the second highest and the CF has the lowest performance. This result can be explained with the restrictions on the path between the users and the items. For example, in the case of the CF the path must contain exactly 3 edges and the type of the edges should be `ItemRating`. Regarding the current configuration, the length of the path of the RS is 5 and the type of the only last edge is restricted. The restriction for the SA is the path length of 5. A more trivial result is that the coverage of the methods grow as the more rating values are contained in the knowledge base.

A minor result of the evaluation is that the graph of the RND shows the minor diagonal.

B. Time need

Spreading activation based methods are computation intense. This is the reason why we also summarize the time need of the examined methods. Table III presents the time need of the methods. Column `Method` contains the method configuration. Columns `10000`, `20000`, `40000` and `200000` contains the time necessary to generate the recommendations to draw the ARoC curves in the `10k`, the `20k`, the `40k` and the `200k` case, respectively. The execution times are the total times of calculating 6 040 recommendations, as the ARoC curve averages the performance of the method among the users in the dataset.

TABLE III. THE TIME NEED OF THE EVALUATION OF THE METHODS IN THE INVOLVED SCENARIOS.

Method	10 000	20 000	40 000	200 000
CF	00:00:28	00:00:50	00:01:22	00:13:46
SA	00:29:07	00:52:38	00:34:20	00:58:05
RS	01:07:44	03:34:08	06:05:55	04:14:30

The numerical experiments have been conducted in a virtualised environment on a single computation core. The virtual hardware configuration is Intel(R) Xeon(R) CPU E5-2650 @ 2.00GHz, 11GB of memory. Regarding the computational resource need, the CF has the highest performance, SA is the next and RS involves the most resources.

VII. CONCLUSION

The performance of collaborative filtering, spreading activation and recommendation spreading is compared on the MovieLens dataset. The methods operate on the knowledge graph presented in Section III. The evaluation is based on ARoC, which evaluation method is introduced in this paper. Its essence is to average the RoC curves over all the users in the dataset. The evaluation results present the ARoC graphs of the methods in three different cases. The evaluation cases are distinguished by the amount of rating information inserted into the knowledge graph.

The SA calculates recommendations based on the structure of the knowledge graph. The CF derives its recommendations from user preferences on items. As its definition shows, recommendation spreading alloys spreading activation and collaborative filtering. On one hand, the RS can be treated as the generalization of the CF for the graph based case. On the other hand, the RS can be treated as the extension of the SA with the ability to incorporate rating values into the recommendations process. The method has the capability to both utilize the structure of the network to stabilize its performance and to involve the explicit ratings as a sophisticated declaration of the user affinity to the recommendable items. To draw a conclusion, the evaluation results show that regarding to the ARoC, while the CF and the SA show a varying performance, the RS successfully alloys the information found in the structure of the network and the information found in the user ratings. The price for the higher recommendation quality is the higher computational resource need.

Thinking about the cold start problem and the information sparse case, we would like to emphasize the evaluation case `1k`. This is the case with the lowest amount of information about user preferences on items. Also, this is the case, when the methods involving the user ratings as an information source provide a better performance than the ranking based spreading activation. To draw a conclusion based on the results, the rating values hold an important source of information, especially in the information sparse environment.

Analysing the ARoC curves over the evaluation cases, the graphs show that the performance of the methods decrease as the more training data is added to the knowledge base. This result lets us draw the same conclusion as described by Blanco-Fernandez et al. [22], as spreading activation based methods have the potential to avoid overspecialization.

In our future work, first of all, we would like to extend the evaluation scenarios to additional datasets. In addition, at the moment, no representation learning techniques are involved in the experiment. In order to further investigate the methods, our plan is to apply SVD or other matrix factorization technique to the adjacency matrix of the network and to involve additional, matrix factorization recommendation techniques to the evaluation.

References

[1] L. Grad-Gyenge, P. Filzmoser, and H. Werthner, "Recommendations on a Knowledge Graph," in *MLRec 2015 : 1st International Workshop on Machine Learning Methods for Recommender Systems*, 2015, pp. 13–20.

[2] A. Tiroshi, S. Berkovsky, M. A. Kâafar, D. Vallet, and T. Kuflik, "Graph-Based Recommendations: Make the Most Out of Social Data." in *UMAP*, ser. Lecture Notes in Computer Science, V. Dimitrova, T. Kuflik, D. Chin, F. Ricci, P. Dolog, and G.-J. Houben, Eds. Springer, pp. 447–458.

[3] K. Lee and K. Lee, "Escaping your comfort zone: A graph-based recommender system for finding novel recommendations among relevant items." *Expert Syst. Appl.*, no. 10, pp. 4851–4858.

[4] S. Lee, S. Park, M. Kahng, and S. goo Lee, "PathRank: Ranking nodes on a heterogeneous graph for flexible hybrid recommender systems." *Expert Syst. Appl.*, no. 2, pp. 684–697.

[5] C.-N. Ziegler and G. Lausen, "Propagation Models for Trust and Distrust in Social Networks," *Information Systems Frontiers*, vol. 7, no. 4-5, pp. 337–358, Dec. 2005.

[6] R. Guha, R. Kumar, P. Raghavan, and A. Tomkins, "Propagation of trust and distrust," in *WWW '04: Proceedings of the 13th international conference on World Wide Web*. New York, NY, USA: ACM, 2004, pp. 403–412.

[7] A. Jøsang, S. Marsh, and S. Pope, "Exploring Different Types of Trust Propagation." in *iTrust*, ser. Lecture Notes in Computer Science, K. Stølen, W. H. Winsborough, F. Martinelli, and F. Massacci, Eds., vol. 3986. Springer, 2006, pp. 179–192.

[8] P. Massa and P. Avesani, "Trust-Aware Collaborative Filtering for Recommender Systems." in *CoopIS/DOA/ODBASE (1)*, ser. Lecture Notes in Computer Science, R. Meersman and Z. Tari, Eds., vol. 3290. Springer, 2004, pp. 492–508.

[9] J. He, "A Social Network-based Recommender System," Ph.D. dissertation, Los Angeles, CA, USA, 2010, aAI3437557.

[10] I. Konstas, V. Stathopoulos, and J. M. Jose, "On Social Networks and Collaborative Recommendation," in *Proceedings of the 32Nd International ACM SIGIR Conference on Research and Development in Information Retrieval*, ser. SIGIR '09. New York, NY, USA: ACM, 2009, pp. 195–202.

[11] I. Guy *et al.*, "Personalized recommendation of social software items based on social relations." in *RecSys*, L. D. Bergman, A. Tuzhilin, R. D. Burke, A. Felfernig, and L. Schmidt-Thieme, Eds. ACM, pp. 53–60.

[12] I. Cantador and P. Castells, *Multilayered Semantic Social Network Modeling by Ontology-Based User Profiles Clustering: Application to Collaborative Filtering*. Berlin, Heidelberg: Springer Berlin Heidelberg, pp. 334–349.

[13] P. Kazienko, K. Musial, and T. Kajdanowicz, "Multidimensional Social Network in the Social Recommender System," *Trans. Sys. Man Cyber. Part A*, vol. 41, no. 4, pp. 746–759, Jul. 2011.

[14] R. Burke, "The Adaptive Web," P. Brusilovsky, A. Kobsa, and W. Nejdl, Eds. Berlin, Heidelberg: Springer-Verlag, ch. Hybrid Web Recommender Systems, pp. 377–408.

[15] X. Yu *et al.*, "Personalized Entity Recommendation: A Heterogeneous Information Network Approach," in *Proceedings of the 7th ACM International Conference on Web Search and Data Mining*, ser. WSDM '14. New York, NY, USA: ACM, pp. 283–292.

[16] R. Catherine and W. Cohen, "Personalized Recommendations Using Knowledge Graphs: A Probabilistic Logic Programming Approach," in *Proceedings of the 10th ACM Conference on Recommender Systems*, ser. RecSys '16. New York, NY, USA: ACM, pp. 325–332.

[17] Q. Hu *et al.*, "HeteroSales: Utilizing Heterogeneous Social Networks to Identify the Next Enterprise Customer," in *Proceedings of the 25th International Conference on World Wide Web*, ser. WWW '16. Republic and Canton of Geneva, Switzerland: International World Wide Web Conferences Steering Committee, pp. 41–50.

[18] P. Kouki, S. Fakhraei, J. Foulds, M. Eirinaki, and L. Getoor, "HyPER: A Flexible and Extensible Probabilistic Framework for Hybrid Recommender Systems," in *Proceedings of the 9th ACM Conference on Recommender Systems*, ser. RecSys '15. New York, NY, USA: ACM, pp. 99–106.

[19] J. M. Alvarez, L. Polo, P. Abella, W. Jimenez, and J. E. Labra, "Application of the Spreading Activation Technique for Recommending Concepts of well-known ontologies in Medical Systems," 2011.

[20] A. Troussov, D. Parra, and P. Brusilovsky, "Spreading Activation Approach to Tag-aware Recommenders: Modeling Similarity on Multidimensional Networks," D. Jannach, W. Geyer, J. Freyne, S. S. Anand, C. Dugan, B. Mobasher, and A. Kobsa, Eds., 2009, pp. 57–62.

[21] Q. Gao, J. Yan, and M. Liu, "A Semantic Approach to Recommendation System Based on User Ontology and Spreading Activation Model," in *NPC Workshops*, J. Cao, M. Li, C. Weng, Y. Xiang, X. Wang, H. Tang, F. Hong, H. Liu, and Y. Wang, Eds. IEEE Computer Society, 2008, pp. 488–492.

[22] Y. Blanco-Fernández, M. L. Nores, A. Gil-Solla, M. R. Cabrer, and J. J. P. Arias, "Exploring synergies between content-based filtering and Spreading Activation techniques in knowledge-based recommender systems." *Inf. Sci.*, vol. 181, no. 21, pp. 4823–4846, 2011.

[23] X. Jiang and A.-H. Tan, "Learning and inferencing in user ontology for personalized Semantic Web search." *Inf. Sci.*, vol. 179, no. 16, pp. 2794–2808, 2009.

[24] T. Hussein, D. Westheide, and J. Ziegler, "Context-adaptation based on Ontologies and Spreading Activation," in *LWA 2007: Lernen - Wissen - Adaption, Halle, September 2007, Workshop Proceedings*, 2007, pp. 361–366.

[25] V. Codina and L. Ceccaroni, "Taking Advantage of Semantics in Recommendation Systems." in *CCIA*, ser. Frontiers in Artificial Intelligence and Applications, R. Alquézar, A. Moreno, and J. Aguilar-Martin, Eds., vol. 210. IOS Press, 2010, pp. 163–172.

[26] J. L. Herlocker, J. A. Konstan, L. G. Terveen, and J. T. Riedl, "Evaluating Collaborative Filtering Recommender Systems," *ACM Trans. Inf. Syst.*, no. 1, pp. 5–53, Jan.

[27] P. Cremonesi, R. Turrin, E. Lentini, and M. Matteucci, "An Evaluation Methodology for Collaborative Recommender Systems," in *Automated solutions for Cross Media Content and Multi-channel Distribution, 2008. AXMEDIS '08. International Conference on*, Nov 2008, pp. 224–231.

[28] A. I. Schein, A. Popescul, L. H. Ungar, and D. M. Pennock, "CROC: A New Evaluation Criterion for Recommender Systems," *Electronic Commerce Research*, no. 1, pp. 51–74.

[29] G. Schröder, M. Thiele, and W. Lehner, "Setting goals and choosing metrics for recommender system evaluations," in *In CEUR Workshop Proc.*, vol. 811, 2011, pp. 78–85.

[30] P. Resnick, N. Iacovou, M. Suchak, P. Bergstorm, and J. Riedl, "GroupLens: An Open Architecture for Collaborative Filtering of Netnews," in *Proc. of ACM 1994 Conference on Computer Supported Cooperative Work*. Chapel Hill, North Carolina: ACM, 1994, pp. 175–186.

[31] B. Hidasi and D. Tikk, "Speeding up ALS learning via approximate methods for context-aware recommendations," *Knowledge and Information Systems*, no. 1, pp. 131–155.

[32] M. R. Quillian, "Semantic memory," in *Semantic Information Processing*, M. Minsky, Ed. Cambridge, MA: MIT Press, 1968, pp. 227–270.

[33] M. Hochmeister, "Spreading Expertise Scores in Overlay Learner Models." in *CSEDU (1)*, M. Helfert, M. J. Martins, and J. Cordeiro, Eds. SciTePress, pp. 175–180.

[34] D. H. Wolpert and W. G. Macready, "No Free Lunch Theorems for Optimization," *Trans. Evol. Comp*, no. 1, pp. 67–82, Apr.

Statistical Sampling in Process Mining Discovery

Alessandro Berti

SIAV
Italy, 35030 Rubano (Padova)
Email: alessandro.berti89@gmail.com

***Abstract*—In this paper, we propose some ideas related to the application of Statistical Sampling techiques to simplify the application of a Process Discovery algorithm to big amounts of data. Much of the information about the business process could be indeed discovered by analyzing only a small amount of events, making useless the application of the algorithm to the entire data set.**

Keywords–Process Mining; Statistical Sampling; Big Data.

I. INTRODUCTION

Process Mining [1][2][3] is related to the discovery of information about business processes, and there are several techniques proposed for Business Process Discovery [4], Business Process Conformance [5], Business Process Prediction [6]. A recent field of research is about the application of Process Mining to big amounts of data [7][8][9]. We can cite some approaches to process discovery using GPU computing [10], Hadoop MapReduce [11], and an approach to streaming process data using Amazon Kinesis [12]. An open question is how much of the collected data is necessary for a Process Discovery algorithm in order to discover the process schema. In this paper, we propose some ideas about the use of statistical sampling to event logs that means applying a Process Discovery algorithm only on some process instances, e.g., a small amount of the collected data. The paper is organized as follows: Section 2 introduces a process discovery algorithm, Section 3 shows a method to apply statistical sampling to the process discovery algorithm introduced in Section 2, in Section 4 there are some measures in order to evaluate the soundness of the approach proposed in Section 3.

II. BACKGROUND

A widely used Process Discovery technique is Heuristics Miner [13][14]. The algorithm, given as input the event log, works calculating a dependency measure between activities:

$$dep(A, B) = |A => B| = \frac{|A > B| - |B > A|}{|A > B| + |B > A| + 1}$$

Where $|A > B|$ is the count of occurrences in the log where an event with activity A is followed by an event with activity B, and $|B > A|$ is the count of occurrences in the log where an event with activity B is followed by an event with activity A. This dependency threshold is comprised between -1 and 1. Activities A and B are considered in *dependency* if $|A => B|$ exceeds a dependency threshold. If two activities A and B are in dependency, then in the resulting process model, there is an edge connecting activity A and activity B.

III. METHOD

Applying the Heuristics Miner process discovery algorithm only to a small subset of the event log, the output might comprise:

- Some activities that are in clear dependency (e.g., the dependency value is very near to 1).
- Some activities that are not in dependency (e.g., the dependency value is below 0).
- Some activities that may be in dependency (might be slightly above or slightly below the dependency threshold).

The question is if the output of the application of Heuristics Miner to the small subset of the log is reliable; that means if the activities are in clear dependency in the small subset, then they are in dependency on the entire event log, and if the activities are not in dependency on the sample, then they are not in dependency on the entire log. We have to examine the following questions:

1) Is the subset of the log a representative sample of the entire log?
2) Is the subset of the log big enough to infer the dependencies?

To avoid taking an unrepresentative sample, random traces in the log should be taken. Indeed, taking the first traces in the log (e.g., the traces that happened first) could be dangerous as there could be a concept drift in the process [15][16]. This could be granted using a random-access storage like Apache HBase [17]. In order to reply to the second question, we have to do some assumptions on the probabilistic distribution of dependency values. If the dependency values calculated on various random-taken subsets of the log follow a normal distribution, then we can define a *confidence interval* on the dependency value between activities A and B, given a sample of size N (in the following formula, we denote with p the value $dep_{sample}(A, B)$), as:

$$dep_{entire}(A, B) \in \left(p - k\sqrt{\frac{p(1-p)}{N}}, p + k\sqrt{\frac{p(1-p)}{N}}\right)$$

Where k is a constant given by the chosen confidence (for example, $k = 1.96$ if we want a 95% confidence). The formula means that the value of dependency on the entire log $dep_{entire}(A, B)$ is comprised (with a confidence given by the value of k) in some interval centered on $dep_{sample}(A, B)$. For $N \to \infty$, e.g., for a big sample size, we can see that the interval length goes to 0 (this means that with a big sample size we get a dependency value that is equal or almost equal to the dependency value measured on the entire log). However, even for a smaller sample, if $dep_{sample}(A, B)$ exceeds by much the dependency threshold, we could be quite sure that also $dep_{entire}(A, B)$ exceeds the dependency threshold, so a small subset of the log is enough to say that A and B are in dependency. Our proposal to determine a good sample size is described in the following algorithm that starts with an empty sample. The algorithm adds iteratively N traces (that are chosen randomly from the log) to the sample until a stop condition is reached; in each step, dependency measures between activities are calculated. The parameters of the algorithm are: N that is the number of traces added in each iteration; p that is described in the previous paragraphs; q that is the probability of doing another iteration of the algorithm.

1) Add N random traces to the sample.
2) Calculate the dependency values (in the sample) between activities.
3) For all activities that are in dependency on the sample, check the value $inf = p - k\sqrt{\frac{p(1-p)}{N}}$.
4) If for all activities that are in dependency on the sample, the value inf is above the dependency threshold, then return the dependency set found on the sample.
5) If there is no couple of activities where the value inf is above the dependency threshold, then do another iteration of the algorithm.
6) Otherwise, do another iteration of the algorithm with probability q and return the dependency set found on the sample with probability $1 - q$.

The output of the previous algorithm is a sample whose size is a multiple of N: if we do m iterations of the algorithm, then the (final) sample size will be mN. The proposed algorithm is probabilistic, as the produced sample is dependent on the traces that are chosen during its execution.

IV. Results and Conclusion

The main assumption we have done on dependencies is that they follow a normal distribution, chosen a random sample of size N. We have checked this assumption (using Kolmogorov-Smirnov) on two event logs: "Road Traffic Fine Management Process" [18] (that contains 150370 traces) and "Receipt phase of an environmental permit application process" [19] (that contains 1434 traces). The process underlying these logs is very regular (it is a "lasagna" process); while the normality of dependencies in less regular, "spaghetti", processes (as "BPI Challenge 2015 Municipality 1" log [20]) is not equally clear.

There are several possible evaluation metrics of the sampling method proposed in the previous section which are based on several executions:

- (*E1*) Average (final) sample size as a fraction of the entire event log. As example, if we have a log with 1000 traces, choose $N = 100$ and, after the execution of the algorithm, we get a sample of size $4*N = 400$, then *E1* $= 0.4$.
- (*E2*) Average percentage of dependencies on the entire log that are dependencies also on the sample.
- (*E3*) Average percentage of dependencies in the sample that are not dependencies on the entire log.

We can propose an evaluation of the algorithm on the "Road Traffic Fine Management Process" and on the "Receipt phase of an environmental permit application process" logs. We have chosen 0.9 as dependency threshold, $k = 1.96$ for the confidence interval and $q = 1.0$ as the probability of doing another iteration of the algorithm. Moreover, we have chosen $N = 1000$ as sample size for "Road Traffic Fine Management Process" and $N = 10$ as sample size for "Receipt phase of an environmental permit application process". As the algorithm is probabilistic (sample size is dependent on which traces are chosen), it has been repeated on both logs for $M = 1000$ trials (Monte Carlo algorithm) averaging the metrics values recorded during the M executions.

For the "Road Traffic Fine Management Process" we have obtained the following values in the average of the proposed metrics: *E1* $= 0.024$, *E2* $= 0.9540$, *E3* $= 0.6154$. For the "Receipt phase of an environmental permit application process" we have obtained the following values in the proposed metrics: *E1* $= 0.0200$, *E2* $= 0.9827$, *E3* $= 0.2468$. So in both cases we can extract averagely over 95 % of the dependencies with less than 3 % of the entire log. Evaluation metric *E3* shows less good values, and some dependencies extracted on the sample are not dependencies on the entire log.

The point behind this paper is that, even if Big Data technology is becoming cheaper, unleashing such power to analyze an event log may not be useful as a small sample could still contain the dependencies we would find on the entire log.

References

[1] W. M. Van der Aalst and A. Weijters, "Process mining: a research agenda," *Computers in industry*, vol. 53, no. 3, pp. 231–244, 2004.

[2] W. M. van der Aalst et al., "Business process mining: An industrial application," *Information Systems*, vol. 32, no. 5, pp. 713–732, 2007.

[3] W. Van Der Aalst et al., "Process mining manifesto," in *International Conference on Business Process Management*. Springer, pp. 169–194, 2011.

[4] J. E. Cook and A. L. Wolf, "Automating process discovery through event-data analysis," in *Proceedings of the 17th international conference on Software engineering*. ACM, pp. 73–82, 1995.

[5] W. M. Van der Aalst and A. K. A. de Medeiros, "Process mining and security: Detecting anomalous process executions and checking process conformance," *Electronic Notes in Theoretical Computer Science*, vol. 121, pp. 3–21, 2005.

[6] W. M. Van der Aalst, M. H. Schonenberg, and M. Song, "Time prediction based on process mining," *Information Systems*, vol. 36, no. 2 pp. 450–475, 2011.

[7] A. Vera-Baquero, R. Colomo-Palacios, and O. Molloy, "Business process analytics using a big data approach," *IT Professional*, vol. 15, no. 6, pp. 29–35, 2013.

[8] W. M. Van Der Aalst, "Decomposing process mining problems using passages," in *International Conference on Application and Theory of Petri Nets and Concurrency*. Springer, pp. 72–91, 2012.

[9] W. van der Aalst, "Process mining in the large," in *Process Mining*. Springer, pp. 353–385, 2016.

[10] J. Zhou, K.-M. Yu, and B.-C. Wu, "Parallel frequent patterns mining algorithm on gpu," in *Systems Man and Cybernetics (SMC), 2010 IEEE International Conference on*. IEEE, pp. 435–440, 2010.

[11] H. Reguieg, F. Toumani, H. R. Motahari-Nezhad, and B. Benatallah, "Using mapreduce to scale events correlation discovery for business processes mining," in *International Conference on Business Process Management*. Springer, pp. 279–284, 2012.

[12] J. Evermann, J.-R. Rehse, and P. Fettke, "Process discovery from event stream data in the cloud–a scalable, distributed implementation of the flexible heuristics miner on the amazon kinesis cloud infrastructure.", 2016

[13] A. Weijters, W. M. van Der Aalst, and A. A. De Medeiros, "Process mining with the heuristics miner-algorithm," *Technische Universiteit Eindhoven, Tech. Rep. WP*, vol. 166, pp. 1–34, 2006.

[14] A. Burattin, "Heuristics miner for time interval," in *Process Mining Techniques in Business Environments*. Springer, pp. 85–95, 2015.

[15] R. J. C. Bose, W. M. van der Aalst, I. Žliobaitė, and M. Pechenizkiy, "Handling concept drift in process mining," in *International Conference on Advanced Information Systems Engineering*. Springer, pp. 391–405, 2011.

[16] J. Carmona and R. Gavalda, "Online techniques for dealing with concept drift in process mining," in *International Symposium on Intelligent Data Analysis*. Springer, pp. 90–102, 2012.

[17] M. N. Vora, "Hadoop-hbase for large-scale data," in *Computer science and network technology (ICCSNT), 2011 international conference on*, vol. 1. IEEE, pp. 601–605, 2011.

[18] de Leoni, Mannhardt, "Road Traffic Fine Management Process". Eindhoven University of Technology. Dataset. http://dx.doi.org/10.4121/uuid:270fd440-1057-4fb9-89a9-b699b47990f5, 2005

[19] Buijs, J.C.A.M., "Receipt phase of an environmental permit application process (WABO)", CoSeLoG project. Eindhoven University of Technology. Dataset. http://dx.doi.org/10.4121/uuid:a07386a5-7be3-4367-9535-70bc9e77dbe6, 2014

[20] B.F. van Dongen, "BPI Challenge 2015 Municipality 1". Eindhoven University of Technology. Dataset. http://dx.doi.org/10.4121/uuid:a0addfda-2044-4541-a450-fdcc9fe16d17, 2015

Support System for Creating Pathfinder Using Reference Examples

Yasuro Nakao
Morioka University, Faculty of Literature, Japan
Morioka, Japan
E-mail: yas@kyudai.jp

Abstract—**A library pathfinder is a guide that gathers basic information resources on a specific subject. However, the library pathfinder is developed using a manual method based on a librarian's experience and present knowledge. Therefore, there is an issue of whether a pathfinder contains suitable resources. In this study, a pathfinder support system has been developed to produce a pathfinder draft using past library reference example data. As a result, it was discovered that the suggestion method developed here could possibly search relevant resources that are not accessible using the Online Public Access Catalog (OPAC) base method.**

Keywords-reference service; library pathfinder; reference example; reference tool; Reference Collaborative Database.

I. Introduction

A library reference service mediates between a user and the information that the user needs. In a conventional library reference service, reference research is conducted after receiving a question from a user, thus making it a passive service.

In contrast, a more active library reference service has been offered in recent years. This service, called transmission-type information service, anticipates users' needs in advance and offers the appropriate information. It has expanded the conventional library reference service.

A. Library Pathfinder

A transmission-type information service includes various services. One of the most characteristic services is a library pathfinder, hereafter referred to as "pathfinder". Pathfinder has been created at the Massachusetts Institute of Technology library in 1969 [1]. Pathfinder is also called an information guide for users. Pathfinders are generally comprised of leaflets.

Pathfinder comprises basic knowledge and selected resources for learners. These resources are restricted to those that the library holds and a user can access. A pathfinder is different from a comprehensive resource list or web link, as it contains the information that summarizes related basic resources and retrieval methods on a specific subject.

However, the standard of the pathfinder does not exist. The style of the pathfinder varies by library type and target user. Libraries devise the form of a pathfinder specifically for the needs of that library. In many libraries, a pathfinder consists of the following elements:

A. Theme
B. Key word and classification number (NDC: Nippon Decimal Classification)
C. Explanation on a theme
D. Basic printed material and network resource
  * Reference book, secondary resource, database
  * Related book, magazine, newspaper, audio-visual data, web site etc.

There is also not a fixed procedure for making a pathfinder. The following is the process that is generally used:

1. Plan of a theme
2. The decision of keywords or classification number
3. Making of explanation sentence on the theme
4. Searching the following resources using the keywords etc., and making a candidate list for pathfinder.
   • Books, journals or audio-visual materials etc. are searched using Online Public Access Catalog (OPAC).
   • Articles of journal or newspaper are searched using index database.
   • Reference books or web resource are searched using reference information site such as NDL Research Navi.
5. Checking each resource and creating a fixed pathfinder list.
6. Making of bibliography information on each resource
7. The design and edit work

Some libraries generate and offer a pathfinder dynamically using a database. However, many libraries provide a pathfinder statically. A pathfinder is often created by librarian using Office software like Microsoft Word manually. Resources are selected using the librarian's experience and knowledge as a professional. The problem is judging whether the pathfinder is appropriate for the situation. There might be useful resources that the librarian cannot find on account of manual searching based on librarian's experience and knowledge. This suggestion is to support or to complement that with reference service data.

B. Related Work

Research work on library pathfinders includes the following: Kashima et al. introduced the pathfinder to Japanese libraries and considered the importance of subject analysis when making a pathfinder [2]. Ito et al. surveyed the current situation of pathfinder use in Japan [3]. Sakajiri and Ito et al. introduced information about actual pathfinder making, maintaining and managing in the National Diet Library [4][5].

Nakashima studied the system of support for a learner making a pathfinder by himself for active learning [6]. Sakai et al. studied the development of the system for users associated with Wikipedia [7]. In this study a support system to generate pathfinder information for librarians was built and its validity was clarified to contribute to pathfinder construction. To our knowledge there are no studies on support for librarians, not for users when they make a pathfinder in Japanese. And we utilize the information of the reference example that was only recorded, more positively to make a pathfinder. This study aims to support the process (2) and (4) in making pathfinder.

II. METHODOLOGY

This study focuses on the use of reference example data to make a pathfinder. Reference examples are information recorded based on past library reference services.

More than one site exhibits reference example data in Japan. Reference example data are available from the Collaborative Reference Database [8] in the National Diet Library, the largest database in Japan. Reference examples are registered with this database by public, school, university, special and national libraries. This database is the de facto standard database in Japan.

A total of 154,127 records were registered as of the end of March 2016. 89,244 records are open to the public. The number of records in the Collaborative Reference Database is increased every year.

The following are the main components of these records.

> Question / Answer / Reference materials / Answering process / Preliminary research / Keywords / NDC / Type of search / Type of subject / Category of questioner / Resolved/Unresolved / Access level / Creation date of case data. There are other elements for data management like Registration number, Registration date and Last update, etc.

It is not possible to directly use a reference example as a pathfinder, as each reference example is individual or personal record. However, the elements included in this example can be used to make one. In particular, resources recorded in the categories of "Answer", "Reference materials", "Keywords", and "NDC" are useful for pathfinder creation.

A total of 82,823 examples were used in this research. These records are open to the public, and were acquired as of August 12, 2015 through Collaborative Reference Database API.

All reference tools were extracted from the 82,823 examples. Reference tool is the information resource used in reference search, such as reference books, network database or web site and so on. Reference examples have two types of tool, printed resources and network resources. The fields used for extraction were "Answer" and "Reference materials". Reference tools also existed in other fields such as "Answering process". However, there is the possibility that irrelevant or inaccurate resources may have been included in these fields, as "Answering process" is the search memo before final answering.

Printed resources, such as reference books are often described using the Japanese character *kagi* (square bracket; Japanese-style quotation marks) in reference example sentences (Fig. 1, Fig. 2 is translation of Fig. 1). Printed resources were extracted using *kagi*. Network resources, such as databases or websites were extracted using an associated Uniform Resource Locator (URL).

Printed resources have been grouped with the first *wakachigaki* chunk. *Wakachigaki* is the practice of separating words in Japanese with spaces. For example, "NihonKokugoDaijiten" and "NihonKokugoDaijiten ver.4" are treated as the same group. Network resources were grouped by domain name.

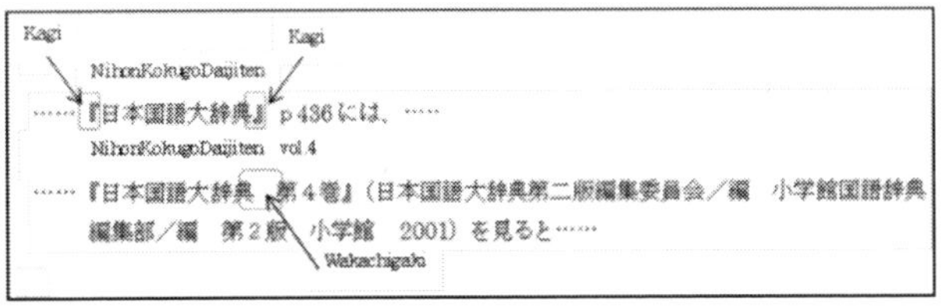

Figure 1. Reference example sentence image. (Japanese)

… the relevant information is in "Complete Japanese-language dictionary" p. 436 …

… according to the "Complete Japanese-language dictionary 2nd edition, the 4th volume" published by Shogakukan in 2001, …

Figure 2. Reference example sentence image (translated into English).

TABLE 1. EXTRACTION DATA.

	Total number	Type number	Number of reference example included (ratio)
Reference tools	246,610	180,826	58,351 (70.5%)
Keywords	195,203	94,259	58,433 (70.6%)
NDC	100,189	848 (section)	59,316 (70.8%)

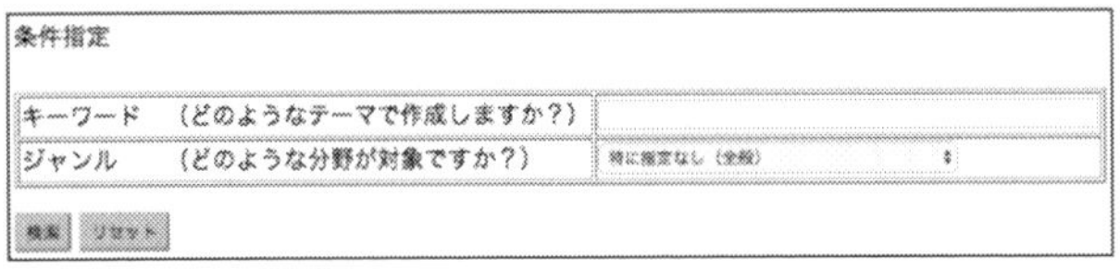

Figure 3. Search screen (Japanese).

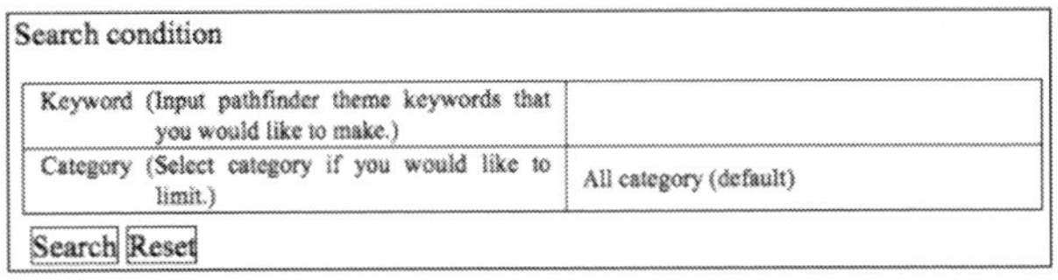

Figure 4. Search screen (translated into English).

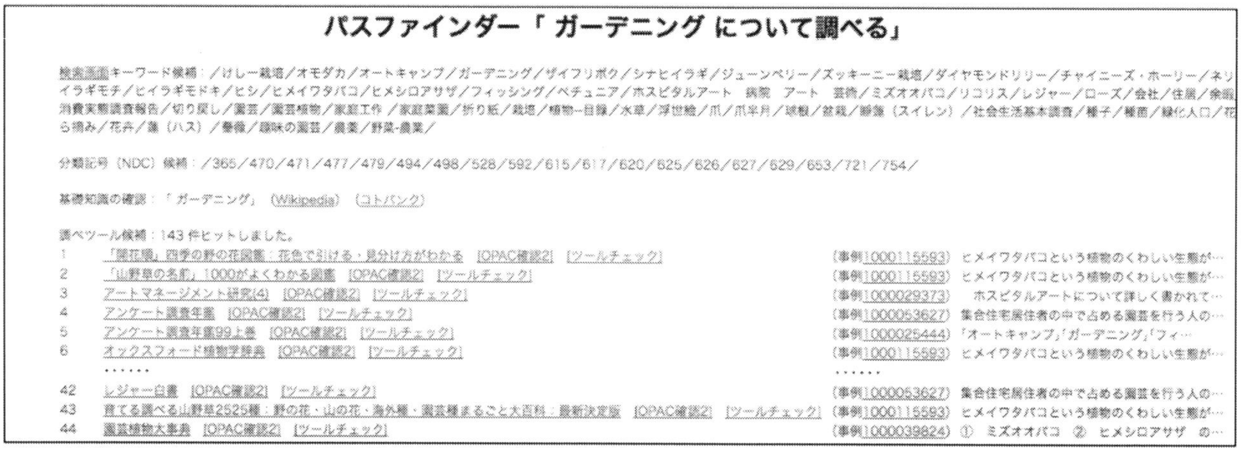

Figure 5. Search results (Japanese).

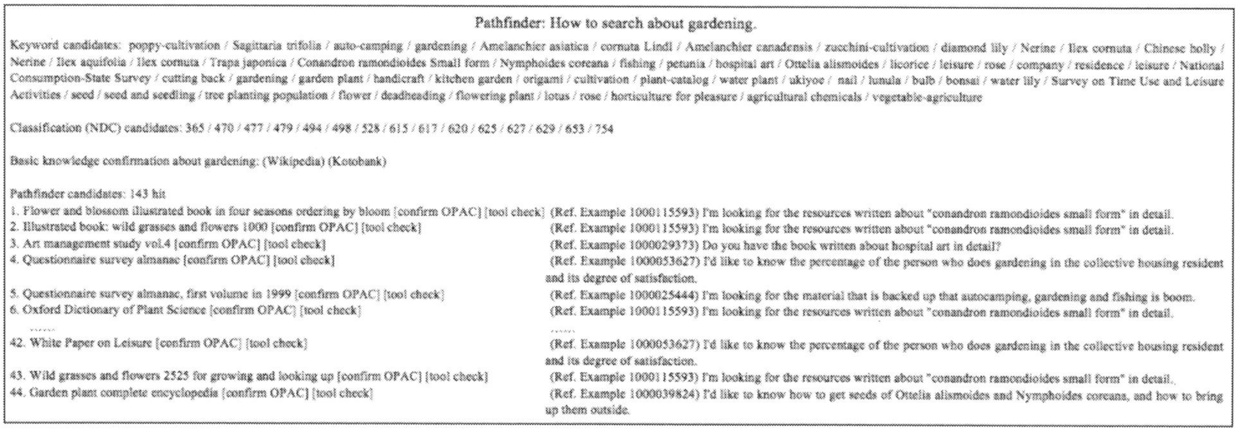

Figure 6. Search results (translated into English).

Keywords were extracted from Keyword fields. NDCs were extracted from NDC fields. Table 1 shows the total data results. A database and prototype search system was built using the extracted data.

The search screen is Japanese as seen in Fig. 3. Fig. 4 is translation of Fig. 3. After submitting search keyword, candidates of related pathfinder resource, keyword and NDC are generated. It is also possible to limit category if necessary using select menu.

The prototype search system is an exact matching system based on keywords. The target fields for searching in this system are "Question", "Answer", "Reference materials" and "Keywords". When entering multiple keywords separated by space, this system searches records including all keywords (AND search).

The search results screen appears as in Fig. 5. Fig. 6 is translation of Fig. 5. The prototype system offers the following functions.

1) Presentation of information resource candidates for the pathfinder.

The set of the reference examples that include search keywords is extracted and the reference tools included in this set are shown as a search result. Search results are divided into printed material and network resource groups. Tools that begin with Hiragana or Katakana are represented in Japanese syllabary order; those beginning with Chinese characters are represented in Chinese-style reading order; and tools that begin with Roman characters are listed in alphabetical order.

2) Presentation of keyword candidates for the pathfinder.

3) Presentation of NDC candidates for the pathfinder.

Keywords and NDCs included in the search results are aggregated and represented.

4) Presentation of questions the reference tool processed and genres the reference tool covered.

When the link "tool check" in Fig. 5 is clicked, Fig. 7 is showed. Fig. 7 is Tool check results window. Fig. 8 is translation of Fig. 7. Tool check results window represents questions that the reference tool processed and genres that the reference tool covered. It is able to confirm reference tool characteristics, all reference examples that the tool used and the genre coverage of NDC class level and division level.

5) Links to the following outside resources:

- Collaborative Reference Database
- Local library OPAC, NDL-OPAC [9]
- NDL Research Navi [10]
- Dictionary or encyclopedia website

When the link "Ref. Example" in Fig. 5 is clicked, the Collaborative Reference Database record that the resource was used is presented. When the link "confirm OPAC" in Fig. 5 is clicked, local OPAC search result is presented. It is able to confirm the holding information of the printed resource. When the each result link in Fig. 5 is clicked, NDL-OPAC search result is presented in the case of printed resource and NDL Research Navi information is presented in the case of network resource. NDL Research Navi is the reference information portal site in Japan. It is able to confirm the bibliographic information of the printed resource, and to confirm the information of the network resource. Dictionary or encyclopedia website, Wikipedia [11] and Kotobank [12] are also linked to confirm further information about the search term. It is able to gather information seamlessly and effectively.

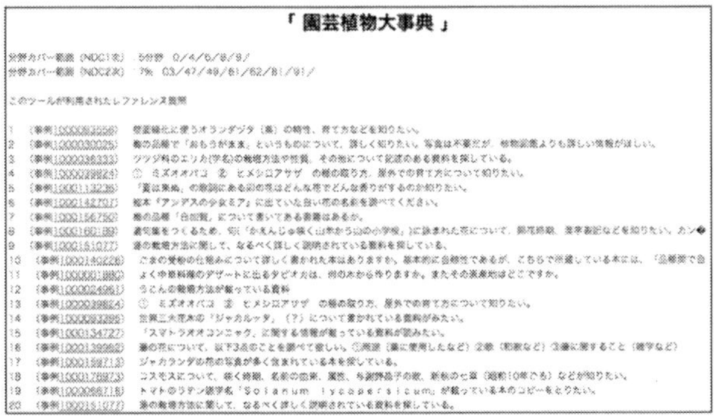
「園芸植物大事典」

Figure 7. Tool check results (Japanese).

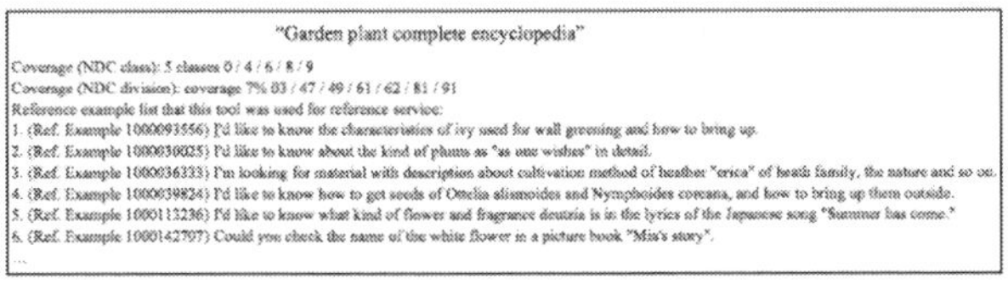
"Garden plant complete encyclopedia"

Coverage (NDC class): 5 classes 0 / 4 / 6 / 8 / 9
Coverage (NDC division): coverage 7% 03 / 47 / 49 / 61 / 62 / 81 / 91
Reference example list that this tool was used for reference service:
1. (Ref. Example 1000093556) I'd like to know the characteristics of ivy used for wall greening and how to bring up.
2. (Ref. Example 1000030025) I'd like to know about the kind of plums as "as one wishes" in detail.
3. (Ref. Example 1000036333) I'm looking for material with description about cultivation method of heather "erica" of heath family, the nature and so on.
4. (Ref. Example 1000039824) I'd like to know how to get seeds of Ottelia alismoides and Nymphoides coreana, and how to bring up them outside.
5. (Ref. Example 1000113236) I'd like to know what kind of flower and fragrance deutzia is in the lyrics of the Japanese song "Summer has come."
6. (Ref. Example 1000142797) Could you check the name of the white flower in a picture book "Mia's story".
...

Figure 8. Tool check results (translated into English).

III. EVALUATION

A library pathfinder is a list of resources selected by the librarian. A pathfinder that includes a wide variety of appropriate resources is useful to users. However it is difficult for even a librarian to pick out the proper resources that the library holds. The prototype system evaluation, therefore, has been performed from the angle of resource discovery. We evaluated how long this system could present the resource that librarian cannot find.

The National Diet Library is exhibiting a pathfinder link between prefectural libraries and government designated city libraries in Japan [13]. First, we investigated the pathfinders exhibited by these libraries and chose 5 themes other than those with specific subjects such as "how to use a database" or subjects limited to the library's local theme. Next, we compared the resources in the result by searching Morioka University Library OPAC [14] that the author belongs to, with keywords matching those provided by the prototype system. Table 2 shows the result.

ROPAC (KW) is the set of resources in the result by searching OPAC with the search keyword KW. RSYSTEM (KW) is the set of resources that the prototype system brings up in the case of using the search keyword KW. R'SYSTEM (KW) is the set of resources that are included in RSYSTEM (KW) and the library holds. ROPAC (KW) ∩ R'SYSTEM (KW) is the set intersection of ROPAC (KW) and R'SYSTEM (KW). R'SYSTEM (KW) − ROPAC (KW) is the set of resources that are included in R'SYSTEM (KW) and are not included in ROPAC (KW). The number of resources in each set is shown in Table 2 under each set name.

The proposed support system retrieves resources that we cannot find by searching OPAC. These include printed resources that are related to the theme of the intended pathfinder. The proposed system, therefore, has the potential to increase appropriate resources for creating a pathfinder.

IV. CONCLUSION AND FUTURE WORK

A reference example has been recorded to accumulate data present in Japanese libraries. Based on previous research, we can assume that by using reference examples, it is possible to find related resources that are difficult to access using an OPAC-based search. Suggestion system using reference examples can expect to complement candidates of resource for the pathfinder. It is possible to increase the reusability of a reference example.

However, we could not judge how useful resources are included from a librarian at this time on account of lacking enough time. It is future's problem to evaluate that. A test at a public library should be conducted next. In particular, the validity of the constructed pathfinder has to be inspected. It is also necessary to validate the function of checking a reference tool and suggesting keywords or NDCs for the pathfinder.

TABLE 2. RESOURCES DISCOVERED USING THE PROTOTYPE.

Pathfinder	*KW* (Search Keyword)	$R_{OPAC}(KW)$	$R_{SYSTEM}(KW)$	$R'_{SYSTEM}(KW)$	$R_{OPAC}(KW) \cap R'_{SYSTEM}(KW)$	$R'_{SYSTEM}(KW) - R_{OPAC}(KW)$
"How to search about fermented food"	Fermented food	24	115	35	2	33
"How to search about developmental disability"	Developmental disability	208	163	30	20	10
"How to search about influenza"	Influenza	21	99	12	1	11
"How to search about the game of Igo"	The game of Igo	9	98	23	2	21
"How to search about The legends of Tono"	The legends of Tono	51	71	30	2	28

REFERENCES

[1] P. M Canfield, "Instructional Materials: Design and Development. Library Pathfinders," Drexel Library Quarterly, vol. 8, pp. 287-300, 1972

[2] M. Kashima and S. Yamaguchi, "Electronic pathfinders: a window to a new generation library service," The Journal of Information Science and Technology Association, vol. 52, no. 10, pp. 526–537, 2002. http://ci.nii.ac.jp/naid/110002826712/ (accessed 2016-07-07)

[3] M. Ito and K. Ozawa, "A research on the existing condition of online library pathfinders in Japan," The Journal of Information Science and Technology Association, vol. 58, no. 7, pp. 361-366, 2008. http://ci.nii.ac.jp/naid/110006793619/ (accessed 2016-07-07)

[4] K. Sakajiri, "RESEARCH NAVI by the National Diet Library: outline of structuring tasks and contents," The Library Journal, vol. 106, no.4, pp. 248–251, 2012. http://ci.nii.ac.jp/naid/40019215521/ (accessed 2016-07-07)

[5] M. Ito and K. Ozawa, "Reference work: Compiling and providing online pathfinders using reference examples: efforts by business, science and technology division, the National Diet Library to provide subject information, and results," Reference service and bibliography, vol. 68, pp. 50-68, 2008. http://ci.nii.ac.jp/naid/40015976209/ (accessed 2016-07-07)

[6] M. Nakashima, "Creating Web-pathfinders Providing Reliability and Convenience in the Format According to the Information-seeking Behavior Model," 2011, https://kaken.nii.ac.jp/en/report/KAKENHI-PROJECT-21500238/RECORD-21500238seika/ (accessed 2016-07-07)

[7] T. Sakai, H. Masuda, Y. Kiyota and Y. Nakagawa, "An Automated Pathfinder System Using Wikipedia and Library Information Resources," Proceedings of the Information Processing Society of Japan Annual Convention, vol. 72, pp.65 - 66, 2010. http://ci.nii.ac.jp/naid/110008139017/ (accessed 2016-07-07)

[8] http://crd.ndl.go.jp/reference/ (accessed 2016-07-07)

[9] https://ndlopac.ndl.go.jp/ (accessed 2016-07-07)

[10] http://rnavi.ndl.go.jp/rnavi/ (accessed 2016-07-07)

[11] https://ja.wikipedia.org/ (accessed 2016-07-07)

[12] https://kotobank.jp/ (accessed 2016-07-07)

[13] http://rnavi.ndl.go.jp/research_guide/pubpath.php (accessed 2016-07-07)

[14] https://morioka-opac.limedio.ricoh.co.jp/mylimedio/search/search-input.do?mode=comp&nqid=1&lang=en (accessed 2016-07-07)

An Analysis of Expression Patterns for Establishing Research Significance

Kiyoko Uchiyama
Dept. Applied Computer Science
Shonan Institute of Technology
Fujisawa, Japan
e-mail: uchiyama@sc.shonan-it.ac.jp

Abstract—**It is crucial to investigate essential information for comprehending contents of technical documents and academic papers in order to write a paper as novices. The previous works revealed the importance of grasping the logical structure and the knowledge of technical terms in the domain-specific field. As it takes a lot of time to acquire the knowledge of technical terms, a method which can be assumed the meaning of technical terms requires for effective reading. In this paper, we attempt to extract and analyze expression patterns of establishing discourse structure and reflecting author's intention in the Section Introduction of academic papers. The analysis carried out using by original categorization based on the existing model and reported the results.**

Keywords-Expression Patterns; Comprehensive Reading; Creating A Research Space (CARS) model.

I. INTRODUCTION

In academic education, some important assignments ask for reading academic papers and writing a report in specific field. Students in the engineering department have a lot of assignments that require reading of academic papers and technical reports related to the state of the art of technology.

Such documents, however, include various technical terms, which are unknown words for undergraduate students. A lack of knowledge of technical terms makes it difficult for novices to read the technical documents in the specific field. On the other hand, education for reading technical documents is not enough at the early stage of research.

We have proposed a method for reading technical documents, understanding technical terms and function words in logical structure. Firstly, regarding the technical terms, novices need to know the technical terms, which are basic and essential to a target field, in advance. However, the importance or essentiality of the terms in a target field remains unclear. We defined such technical terms as introductory terms. If novices do not have any knowledge of the introductory terms, they cannot comprehend the outline nor understand more difficult terms in a target field. We proposed various criteria for identifying the terms in a specific domain [1]. We proposed original criteria for the introductory terms: priority and compositionality and calculated the score based on C-Value [2]. C-Value is one of the term scoring methods and uses the type and token frequency for each constituent from the compound nouns in a corpus of the target field.

At first, we defined priority as a sort of ordering for learning in textbooks and attractive keywords in research papers. Secondly, concerning the compositionality, introductory terms tend to generate various new compound nouns by concatenating single words or word strings in prefix/suffix form. The introductory term candidates were calculated based on the type and token frequency occurred in academic papers and textbooks. As the result, we found that the frequency from the table of contents in textbooks was useful for extracting the introductory terms.

The subsequent analysis of the distribution of the terms has processed in a logical structure, such as "Abstract", "Introduction", and "Conclusion" [3]. The introductory terms tend to be included in the logical structure of "Abstract" and "Introduction", rather than that of "Experiment", "Discussion" and "Conclusion". It is assumed that novices can understand the outline of technical documents by effective reading the section of "Abstract" and "Introduction".

Based on those previous analysis, comprehensive reading in "Abstract" and "Introduction" section is necessary for novices in order to grasp the outline of the target paper effectively. As the "Abstract" section is too short to analyze the structure, "Introduction" is a target section.

As it takes a lot of time to acquire the knowledge of the technical terms in a specific field, a method requires other clues for comprehensive reading than the method by using the knowledge of technical term. That is to say, it is crucial that the meaning of technical terms can be detected by using functional words, phrases which establish the author's intention in the context.

In this paper, the expression patterns which reflect the discourse of the paper and the author's intention are analyzed in the context of the Section Introduction. The three steps are introduced for the analysis. Firstly, the role assigned to each sentence, in other words, discourse segment which dominates the context in the paper is processed. Secondly, based on the CARS model (detailed in Section 2), the following three types of expressions, which are related to construction and context of the paper are categorized for this analysis. Three types are (1) mutual expressions frequently used in academic field, (2) characteristic expressions in domain-specific field, and (3) reflecting expressions for establishing the author's intention. Finally, we analyze the relationship between the role of sentence and each type of expressions and organize the results by the previous two steps.

This paper is structured as follows. In Section 2, related works are summarized and our motivation to conduct our study. The analysis and results are described in Section 3 and Section 4 concludes our possible future work.

II. Related Works

There are several researches of rhetorical structure and writing strategy in academic papers. The existing researches are focusing on the role of each sentence and categorization of discourse segmentation related to our research.

A. Creating a Research Space (CARS) model

Based on existing analysis of the Section Introduction, we assumed that the CARS model proposed by Swales [4] can be applied to analyze the structure of target documents. CARS model consists of three moves that describe how research paper introductions are structured.

The three rhetorical moves are: (1) establishing a territory, (2) establishing a niche, and (3) occupying the niche. The model breaks down each of those moves into more detailed descriptions. The move1 establishing a territory includes three steps, claiming centrality, making topic generalizations, and reviewing items of previous research. After describing move1, authors try to write their refutation to earlier research, indicate a gap, raise a question and continue a tradition. Finally, authors reveal their findings or solution to help fill the gap in move2, by outlining purposes, announcing present research and main findings, indicating structure of the paper and evaluation of findings.

In establishing a niche of CARS model, authors claim their research advantages by showing that the previous research are not enough. Authors criticize the existing research by using words expressing a contrast evaluation, such as "less", "little", "fail", "ignore" and "inefficient". This sort of expressions might become clue words for novices to understand the author's intention and find the originalities of the target documents.

B. The Role of Sentence in Discourse Segment

Swales' CARS model has been used extensively by discourse analysis and annotation scheme for information retrieval of scientific papers. A Core Scientific Concepts (CoreSC) is one of the annotation schemes [5][6]. This annotation scheme adopts the view that a scientific paper is the human-readable representation of a scientific investigation. The CoreSC introduced 11 categories. Similarly, de Waad and Pander Maat categorized seven discourse segments: Fact, Problem, Goal, Method, Result, Implication and hypothesis [7][8]. The seven categories at the sentence level can be used for classifying the sentence in the Section Introduction.

We correspond Swales' CARS model to seven discourse segments in each sentence for analyzing expression patterns in the Section Introduction.

III. Analysis and Result

We collected and analyzed academic papers in order to investigate the expressions which are structured. The Section Introduction were selected from the full text of the academic papers. The key expressions were extracted referring Swales' CARS model and classified by the role in structure of Introduction.

A. Target Documents

One hundred academic papers written in Japanese which include a keyword "Natural Language Processing" in Information Processing Journal of Japan from 1998 to 2011 were collected. The 2000 sentences in the Section Introduction are target for this paper. The seven categories of annotation scheme for discourse segments is assigned to each sentence.

B. Analysis and Result

We analyzed three types of expressions. The first type is mutual expressions frequently used in academic field. This type can also define the role of sentence. For example, the expressions like "the purpose of this paper", "we propose a method..." can be assigned the role of "Goal" to the sentences. The second type is characteristic expressions in domain-specific field. There are several kinds of words: clue words in wide range of field, such as "precision" "method" "automation" in information processing or engineering field., domain-specific technical terms which can be defined as introductory terms in our research, such as "morphological analysis" "parse" "corpus" in natural language processing field.

The third type is reflecting expressions for establishing the author's intention which corresponds to Swale's move 2: establishing a niche. The expressions include various part of speech, conjunction, adverbs, verbs and adjectives. The authors tend to use positive/negative words in each part of speech for describing their intention or emphasis point of their research. The words, such as "versatile", "enormous", "redundant", "robust" and "exclusive" are observed characteristically in information processing field. Those expressions are commonly used for evaluating proposed method or research in contrast to the expressions "contrast or negative evaluation" widely used in academic field.

IV. Conclusion

In this study, we defined the expressions which constitute of context and the Section Introduction in academic paper as "establishing expressions". The three steps were proceeded for analysis of each sentence applying the framework of Swale's CARS model and discourse segments. The results of the analysis were that establishing expressions have common ones in academic field and specific ones in domain-specific field. We plan to further investigate the establishing expressions in some field, and confirm whether those expressions can be useful for effective reading.

References

[1] K. Uchiyama, "A Study for Identifying Domain-Specific Introductory Terms in Research Papers," Proc. 9th Terminology and Artificial Intelligence, pp.147-150, 2011.
[2] Katerina T. Frantzi and Sophia Ananiadou (1996). Extracting Nested Collocations, In proceedings of the 16th International Conference on Computational Linguistics (COLING 96):41-46.
[3] K. Uchiyama, "An Analysis of Domain-Specific Introductory Terms in Logical Structure of Scholarly Papers," Proc. Workshop on Corpus Japanese Linguistics, pp. 195-198, 2012.
[4] J. Swales, Genre Analysis English in Academic and Research settings, Cambridge University press, 1990.
[5] M. Liakata, S. Teufel, A. Siddharthan, and C. Batchelor, "Corpora for Conceptualization and Zoning of Scientific Papers," Proc. Language Resources and Evaluation (LREC2010), pp.2054-2061, 2010.
[6] M. Liakata, S. Saha, S. Dobnik, C. Batchelor, and D. R. Schuhmann, "Automatic Recognition of Conceptualization Zones in Scientific Articles and Two Life Science Applications," Bioinformatics, 28(7), pp.991-1000, 2012.
[7] A. de Waard and H. P. Maat., "Categorizing Epistemic Segment Types in Biology Research Articles," Proc. Workshop on Linguistic and Psycholinguistic Approaches to Text Structuring (LPTS 2009), 2009.
[8] A. de Waard and H. P. Maat, "Epistemic modality and knowledge attribution in scientific discourse: a taxonomy of types and overview of features," Proc. Workshop on Detecting Structure in Scholarly Discourse, pp.47-55, 2012.

Benchmarking Mi-NER: Malay Entity Recognition Engine

Thenmalar Ulanganathan[1], Ali Ebrahimi[1], Benjamin Chu Min Xian[3], Khalil Bouzekri[1],
Rohana Mahmud[2], Ong Hong Hoe[1]
[1]Artificial Intelligence Lab
MIMOS Berhad
Malaysia
email: thenmalar.nathan | ali.ebrahimi | khalil.ben | hh.ong@mimos.my
[2]Department of Artificial Intelligence
Faculty of Computer Science & Information Technology
University of Malaya
rohanamahmud@um.edu.my
[3]benjamin-chu@live.com

Abstract— **Named entity recognition (NER) is a process of recognizing, identifying, and extracting useful entities, like person, location and organization for information mining from unstructured texts. This paper presents (Mi-NER), a Malay language Named Entity Recognition engine that is developed using a probabilistic approach. The results of benchmarking Mi-NER against existing systems are presented in this paper. In addition, the details of the experimental work are highlighted and discussed. Precision, Recall and F-Measure have been used to measure the results for this evaluation.**

Keywords-Benchmarking; Malay Language; Natural Language Processing; Named Entity Recognition.

I. INTRODUCTION

In recent years, development in semantic analysis of unstructured text has triggered many applications in Text Mining, Summarization, Text Understanding, Information Retrieval and Extraction [1][2].

Named Entity Recognition (NER) is a subtask of information extraction which involves identification of proper nouns in texts, called named entities, and classification of these named entities into a set of pre-defined categories of interest (e.g., Person, Location, Organization) [3]. The main goal of NER is to reduce the manual annotation of named entities in texts by human annotator which is a time-consuming and laborious process. However, in order to automate this process, machines have to be trained, as they need to analyze and understand the content of the text before being able to recognize the named entities. Machine learning techniques including statistical and probabilistic methods have been used to successfully build automated NER engines [4]-[7].

Building a machine learning model necessitates an NER-annotated corpus to be able to detect the correct entity types for new words/phrases based on the context. Such corpora are available for the major languages, such as English, Chinese, Spanish, and Hindi [8]. However, due to the lack of linguistic resources for Malay language, training corpora have to be built from scratch to train NER models. In this paper, a Malay NER engine called Mi-NER is presented and compared with existing Malay NER engines. A manually-built corpus is used to train the NER model. Another two manually-built corpora are used to test the models.

This paper is structured as follows: Section 2 describes the related work on existing NER systems; Section 3 highlights the proposed Machine Learning model of Mi-NER; Section 4 shows the experimental results; Section 5 discusses the results of Mi-NER compared to the existing systems. Finally, Section 6 concludes this paper.

II. RELATED WORK

NER systems exist for various languages, such as English, Dutch, Arabic, Chinese, etc. but only few can be found for Malay language.

In their work, Fong, Y. S. et al. [9] use several text processing modules from A Nearly-New Information Extraction (ANNIE) system. They proposed a method for creating rules and gazetteers for Iban language which is one of the 63 indigenous languages of Sarawak, Malaysia, according to the Dewan Bahasa dan Pustaka (Institute of Language and Literature DBP) [10]. The system includes a tokenizer, a manually-built gazetteer (entity dictionary), a sentence splitter and a part-of-speech (POS) tagger and the use of several rules written with Java Annotation Pattern Engine (JAPE). In this work, rules are designed to detect several named entities including Person, Organization, and Location, as well as other types of entities, such as Time, Monetary, Date and Percentage.

Sharum, M. Y. et al. [11] use a name index and regular expressions to recognize entities only limited to people's names from Malay texts. Therefore, by focusing on minimal techniques of NER to recognize people's names, they showed that the approach of recognizing people's names can be performed and returns precise results. On the other hand, Rayner Alfred et al. in [12] use rule-based approach to identify named entities in Malay texts. The approach uses Rule-Based Part of Speech (RPOS) tagger, which is Malay

Rule-Based POS tagger that applies a POS tag dictionary and affixing rules in order to identify the word definition [12]. The work revolves around designing rules based on the POS tags. For instance, when the POS tag for a particular word is referring to a proper noun, then a specific rule will be applied to this word in order to determine whether it is a named entity or not. In this work, these rules are designed to detect three major types of named entities, which are Person, Organization and Location.

Semantria [13] is able to process Malay texts and its NER feature is able to automatically extract proper nouns like persons, places, or companies from texts. It comprises of a POS module to tag each of the word tokens with a corresponding POS tags. Subsequently, it performs a series of algorithms to extract relevant named entities from texts [13].

In this paper, we compare the results generated from Mi-NER against the results from Rule-Based NER system in [12] and Semantria [13] for our experimental evaluation.

III. ENTITY RECOGNITION MODEL

Natural language Processing (NLP) uses Linear-Chain Conditional Random Fields (Linear-Chain CRF) in many sub sequential text processing task including NER, POS, and word segmentation [14]. Mi-NER uses Linear-Chain CRF machine learning technique to train its NER model [14]. CRF is a popular probabilistic method for structured prediction. It is a technique which has been applied to several domains including bioinformatics, computer vision and text processing. Sha and Pereira [15] created one of the first large-scale applications of CRFs by matching state-of-the-art performance on segmenting noun phrases in text.

After that, linear chain CRFs has been applied on variety of problems in NLP including NER. In NER models, all of the named entity labels are independent. However, the named entity labels of neighboring words are dependent (e.g., Los Angeles: location, Los Angeles Times: organization). One way to relax this independence assumption is to arrange the output variables in linear chains which are CRF.

A. *Training*

In this work, we extracted data from news and non-news sources, respectively Bernama [16] news archive and social media (including tweets, blogs and wikis). Those two sources are used in order to build a training corpus which contains a total of 275,322 tokens. 70% of the training set is collected from news and the remaining part is reserved for non-news. The data is annotated by native speakers and verified by two linguistic experts.

The process of building Malay NER model is further described in Fig. 1. There are three main steps including Preprocessing, Annotation and Generation.

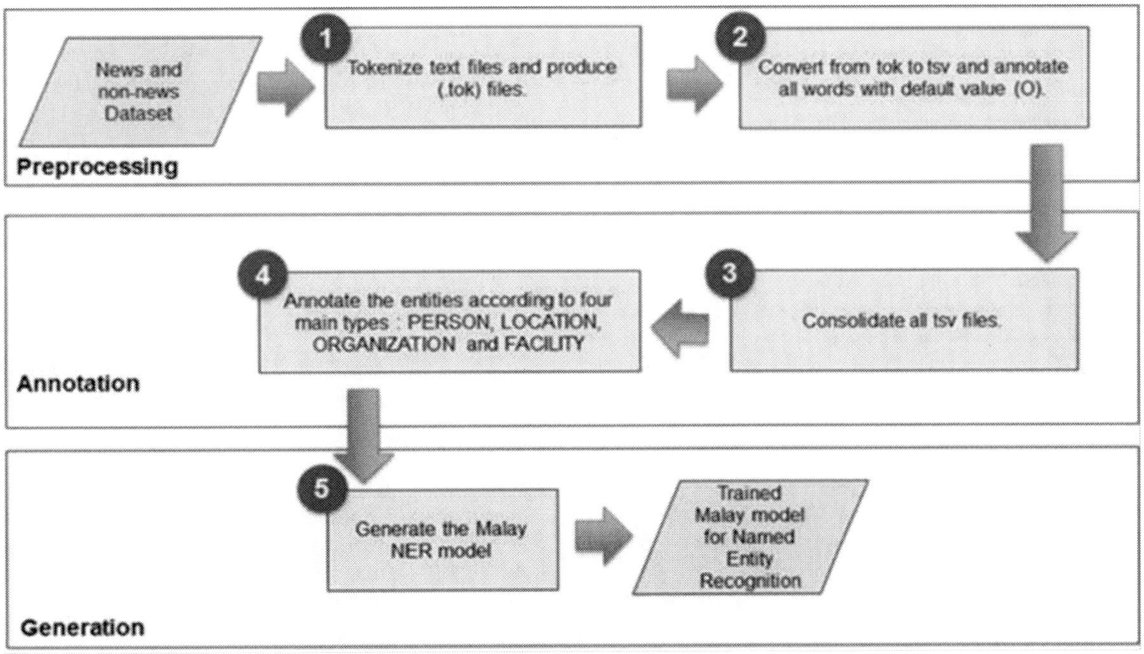

Figure 1. Malay Named Entity Recognition Model Training Process

In the Preprocessing phase, we run the tokenizer to generate a ".tok" file with a token per line. Subsequently, another script is executed to generate a ".tsv" file (Tab Separated Values) where all of these tokens are initialized with a default value "O" (refer Fig. 2). The ".tsv" file is used by Malay native speakers to annotate which are the relevant named entities based on the sentence context. However, ".tsv" file format allows us to save data in which tokens and their entity types are separated by Tab. Four named entity types are considered: PERSON, LOCATION, ORGANIZATION and FACILITY. The output is shown in Fig. 3.

```
1  Diyana→ O↓
2  mengajakO↓
3  Rasyid→ O↓
4  pergi→  O↓
5  ke→     O↓
6  pasar→  O↓
7  di→     O↓
8  Jalan→  O↓
9  Haji→   O↓
10 Sirat→  O↓
11 .→      O↓
12 Azri→   O↓
13 mengajak→       O↓
14 Raizah→ O↓
15 pergi→  O↓
16 ke→     O↓
17 pasar→  O↓
```

Figure 2. TSV file with initialized value

```
1  Diyana→ B-PERSON↓
2  mengajak→       O↓
3  Rasyid→ B-PERSON↓
4  pergi→  O↓
5  ke→     O↓
6  pasar→  O↓
7  di→     O↓
8  Jalan→  B-LOCATION↓
9  Haji→   I-LOCATION↓
10 Sirat→  I-LOCATION↓
11 .→      O↓
12 Azri→   B-PERSON↓
13 mengajak→       O↓
14 Raizah→ B-PERSON↓
15 pergi→  O↓
16 ke→     O↓
17 pasar→  O↓
```

Figure 3. Annotated TSV file by Malay native speakers

The "B" notation is used before any named entity type to represent the beginning element for the named entity. If the name entity contains only one element, "B" notation will represent the beginning as well as ending of the element. Otherwise, if there is more than one element (token) in that named entity, an "I" notation will be assigned to the subsequent token(s) as shown in Fig. 3 (for example, Jalan Haji Sirat).

There are some terms/words which may be used for different purposes. A case in point would be the name entity "Tun Razak" which is a name used to call a person (commonly known as former prime minister of Malaysia as well as his son who is current prime minister), location entity (Jalan Tun Razak) as well as a facility entity(Universiti Tun Abdul Razak).

B. Testing

To benchmark the accuracy of the proposed Mi-NER, two collections of tokenized datasets have been created. These two annotated Malay datasets consist of 500 articles from news and non-news sources with 250 articles in each source, for a total of 8649 tokens for the first dataset and 9077 tokens for the second dataset. The articles for the first dataset are extracted from Harian Metro [17] and Utusan Malaysia news archive [18], whereas the second dataset contains selected articles from the Malay dataset developed in [19] by Su'ad Awab, which consists of different categories including art, economics, education, health, information technology, law, literature, sport, and science.

Both datasets are built in the same way as the training dataset (refer Fig. 1). After that, the results are checked and verified by another two linguistic experts. The final results are used as our gold standard to evaluate the results of the proposed Mi-NER engine, rule-based NER engine [12] and Semantria [13].

IV. EXPERIMENTS AND RESULTS

The results of Mi-NER are compared against the rule-based Malay ER proposed in [12] and Semantria [13].

Precision, Recall and F-Measure

CoNLL-2002 [20] shared task is the established approach of evaluating NER systems by using the following measures: Precision, Recall and F-measure. The precision measures the percentage of entities found by the algorithm that are correct. Recall is based on the percentage of named entities defined in the corpus that were found by the evaluation program. F-measure is used to measure the accuracy of precision and recall measures. F-measure can be interpreted as a weighted average of the precision and recall.

Fig. 4 shows the Precision, Recall and F-measure scores resulting from our evaluation of these systems for news dataset. Mi-NER demonstrated highest Precision with the value of 89.87% followed by Rule-Based ER with 78.95% and Semantria with 52.74%. Mi-NER and Rule-Based ER have almost similar F-measure scores, but generally Rule-Based ER performs better in Recall. Semantria has the lowest scores compared to the rest for Precision, Recall and F-measure.

Fig. 5 displays the Precision, Recall and F-measure scores resulting from our evaluation of the three systems for non-news dataset. As can be seen in Fig. 5, Mi-NER demonstrated highest Precision, Recall and F-measure score with the value of 83.01%, 64.44% and 72.56% respectively. For this dataset, Mi-NER performs better than Rule-Based ER for all the scores. Semantria has the lowest scores compared to the rest for Precision 41.53%, Recall 12.69% and F-measure 19.44%.For this dataset, Mi-NER performs better than Rule-Based ER for all the scores. Semantria has the lowest scores compared to the rest for Precision 41.53%, Recall 12.69% and F-measure 19.44%.

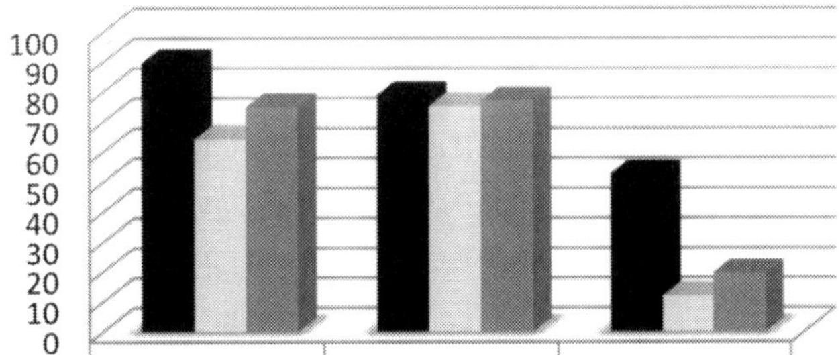

	Mi-ER	Rule Based	Semantria
Precision	89.87	78.95	52.74
Recall	64.33	75.2	12
F-Measure	74.98	77.03	19.56

Figure 4. News Dataset Evaluation Results

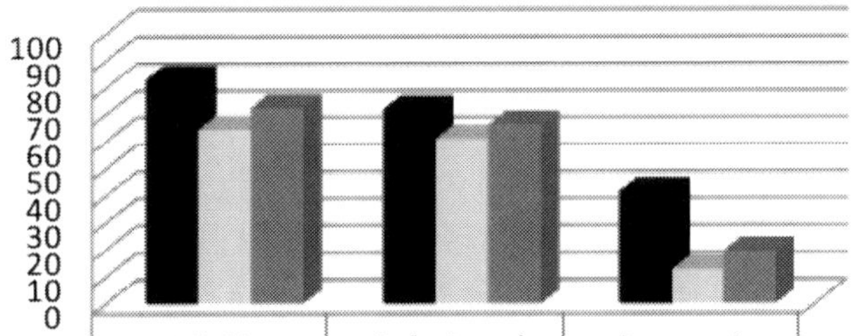

	Mi-ER	Rule Based	Semantria
Precision	83.01	72.13	41.53
Recall	64.44	60.93	12.69
F-Measure	72.56	66.06	19.44

Figure 5. Non-News Dataset Evaluation Results

Fig. 6 illustrates the Precision, Recall and F-measure scores specifically in terms of Person, Location and Organization entities comparing each system in our evaluation for news dataset. Referring to the data in Fig. 6, generally Mi-NER performs better than Rule-Based ER in terms of recognizing Person entities but Rule-Based ER performs better than Mi-NER in recognizing Location and Organization entities for both Recall and F-measure scores. On the other hand, Semantria has the lowest scores for all Precision, Recall and F-measure for recognizing Person, Location and Organization entities.

Fig. 7 represents the Precision, Recall and F-measure scores specifically in terms of Person, Location and Organization entities comparing each system in our evaluation for non-news dataset. Based on the results, generally Mi-NER performs better than Rule-Based ER in terms of recognizing Person and Organization entities but Rule-Based ER performs better than Mi-NER in recognizing Location entities for Recall and F-measure scores. On the other hand, Semantria has the lowest scores for all Precision, Recall and F-measure for recognizing Person, Location and Organization entities.

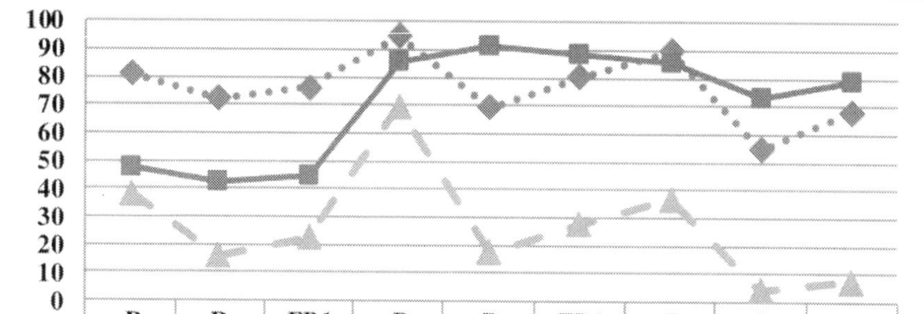

	P (PER)	R (PER)	FB1 (PER)	P (LOC)	R (LOC)	FB1 (LOC)	P (ORG)	R (ORG)	FB1 (ORG)
Mi-NER	80.95	72.12	76.28	94.64	69.37	80.06	89.76	54.76	68.02
Rule-Based	47.62	42.42	44.87	85.75	91.36	88.47	85.37	72.92	78.65
Semantria	38.24	15.76	22.32	69.47	17.28	27.67	36.84	4.17	7.49

Figure 6. News Corpus Analysis for Person(PER), Location (LOC), and Organization(ORG). P: Precision, R: Recall, FB1: F-Measure

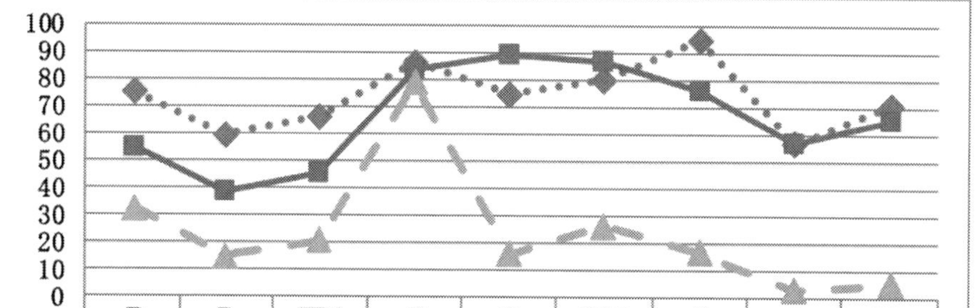

	P (PER)	R (PER)	FB1 (PER)	P (LOC)	R (LOC)	FB1 (LOC)	P (ORG)	R (ORG)	FB1 (ORG)
Mi-NER	75.12	59.45	66.37	86.49	74.77	80.2	94.77	56.86	71.07
Rule-Based	54.75	38.58	45.27	83.84	89.72	86.68	76.53	57.25	65.5
Semantria	32.76	14.96	20.54	79.07	15.89	26.46	16.67	3.05	5.16

Figure 7. Non-news Corpus Analysis for Person(PER), Location (LOC), and Organization(ORG). P: Precision, R: Recall, FB1: F-Measure

V. DISCUSSION

Experiments conducted show that Mi-NER has the highest precision for both the datasets and the highest recall and F-measure scores when tested using the non-news dataset. Experiments also show that the recall of Mi-NER is almost the same for both datasets. However, the Rule-Based ER has a noticeably better recall for the news dataset and thus a higher F-measure score.

Based on the results presented in Fig. 6 and Fig. 7, Mi-NER has the best results for detecting Person entities for both datasets. In fact, all types of entities (i.e., Persons, Locations and Organizations) are detected by Mi-NER with roughly close values. This is mainly because Mi-NER is trained equally on the different types of entities unlike the case of other NER systems. For example, the Rule-Based ER has significantly higher scores for locations and organizations. This is because it supports the detection of locations and organizations with additional dictionaries containing large numbers of locations and organizations to be detected. The dictionaries in addition to the rules used to detect locations and organizations significantly boost the scores for these types. Persons are detected in the Rule-Based ER using only the available rules which fail to cover all possible person names. As a result, the Rule-Based ER detects locations better than Mi-NER. However, Mi-NER outperforms the Rule-Based ER in terms of detecting organizations for the non-news dataset as shown in Fig. 7. News dataset is expected to have a large number of organization entities unlike the non-news dataset. This also affects the training of Mi-NER where it has a higher chance to learn features about fewer numbers of organizations in the non-news dataset.

Semantria locates entities using a Malay POS tagger and a predefined set of entities. Its list of entities can be customized by user's queries to detect the entities that most concern the user. Results show that Semantria has the lowest figures for both datasets. This can be due to problems with the used Malay POS tagger or limitations in the list of entities for Malay language. However, it shows a high precision of detecting locations which indicates that Semantria uses a rich list with sufficient number of location entities unlike other entity types.

Based on our finding, one of the advantages of Mi-NER is to detect the organizations based on the short forms of their suffix like "Sdn" as the short form of Sendirian and "Bhd" as the short form of Berhad and etc. The strategy to add more variation of different types of organization's suffix would enable the system to be more powerful in order to find Person and Organization entities. This strategy applied for Person entities by adding more people's name with different salutations, such as Dato, Datuk, Dato Seri, Datuk Seri, etc. This strategy helps Mi-NER system to differentiate the Location and Person entities, as some persons' name are assigned for a location and by introducing a variety of salutations, Mi-NER system is able to get better results for these cases.

VI. CONCLUSION

In this paper, we have presented a Linear-Chain CRF machine learning technique to train Mi-NER model and benchmark against the rule-based Malay NER proposed in [12] and Semantria [13].

From a qualitative comparison point of view, Mi-NER performs better on the Precision, yet it needs more improvement on the Recall. However, we showed that a statistical approach to develop a NER Engine performs better on some aspects of NER than other rule-based entity recognizers especially when using a large corpus for training. However, there are some challenges with building Malay NER model which caused by lack of online linguistic resources including Malay words have many derivative words that change the syntactic meaning as well as insufficient and limited digital resources. Those factors may restrict applying of machine learning methods and semantic approaches.

Consequently, some improvement will be made especially to improve the current results of Mi-NER in terms of recall by training the model with different variations of sentences.

ACKNOWLEDGMENT

We would like to acknowledge Miss Amiera Syazreen Mohd Ghazali, research assistant at MIMOS Berhad who has contributed to the process of annotating training and testing datasets used in Mi-NER systems. We are also grateful to Dr. Rayner Alfred, associate professor of Computer Science, University Malaysia Sabah and Leow Chin Leong, University Malaysia Sabah for their help to evaluate their Rule-Based ER system on our testing dataset.

REFERENCES

[1] S.Jusoh and H.M. Alfawareh, "Techniques, applications and challenging issue in text mining," International Journal of Computer Science Issues(IJCSI), vol.9, no.6 , pp. 431-436, 2012.

[2] J.Steinberger and K. Jezek, "Using latent semantic analysis in text summarization and summary evaluation," in Proc. ISIM'04, pp. 93-100, 2004.

[3] S.A. Golder and B.A. Huberman, "Usage patterns of collaborative tagging systems", Journal of Information Science, vol.32, no.2, pp. 198-208, 2006.

[4] K.P. Murphy, Machine learning: a probabilistic perspective. 2012: MIT press.

[5] C.Malarkodi, R. Pattabhi and L.D. Sobha. "Tamil ner–coping with real time challenges," in 24th International Conference on Computational Linguistics, pp. 23, 2012.

[6] R. Vijayakrishna and S.L. Devi, "Domain Focused Named Entity Recognizer for Tamil Using Conditional Random Fields," in IJCNLP, pp. 59-66, 2008.

[7] J. Piskorski, "Named-entity recognition for Polish with SProUT," in Intelligent Media Technology for Communicative Intelligence, Springer. p. 122-133,2005.

[8] C. Neudecker, "An Open Corpus for Named Entity Recognition in Historic Newspapers," in Proceedings of the Tenth International Conference on Language Resources and Evaluation (LREC 2016). 2016. Portorož, Slovenia: European Language Resources Association (ELRA).

[9] Y.S. Fong, B. Ranaivo-Malançon and A.Y. Wee. "NERSIL-the Named-Entity Recognition System for Iban Language," in PACLIC, pp. 549-558, 2011.

[10] D.B.d. Pustaka, Malay for The Institute of Language and Literature. 2016; Available from: http://prpm.dbp.gov.my/.

[11] M.Y. Sharum, M.T. Abdullah, M.N. Sulaiman, M.A.A. Murdan and Z.A.A. Hamzah, "Name extraction for unstructured Malay text," in Computers & Informatics (ISCI),IEEE Symposium on. IEEE, pp. 787-791, 2011.

[12] R. Alfred, et al. "A Rule-Based Named-Entity Recognition for Malay Articles," in International Conference on Advanced Data Mining and Applications. Springer, pp.288-299, 2013.

[13] https://www.lexalytics.com/. Semantria., Available from: https://www.lexalytics.com/semantria, Retrieved September, 2016.

[14] A. Culotta, A. McCallum and J. Betz. "Integrating probabilistic extraction models and data mining to discover relations and patterns in text," in Proceedings of the main conference on Human Language Technology Conference of the North American Chapter of the Association of Computational Linguistics. Association for Computational Linguistics, pp. 296-303, 2006.

[15] F. Sha and F. Pereira. "Shallow parsing with conditional random fields," in Proceedings of the 2003 Conference of the North American Chapter of the Association for Computational Linguistics on Human Language Technology-Volume 1. Association for Computational Linguistics, pp.134-141, 2003.

[16] BERNAMA. BERNAMA Archived News, Available from: http://www.bernama.com/bernama/v8/newsarchive.php, 2015.

[17] H. Metro, My Metro, Available from: http://www.hmetro.com.my/, Retrieved September, 2016.

[18] U. Utusan., Utusan Online, Available from: http://www.utusan.com.my/, Retrieved September, 2016.

[19] T. Baldwin and S. Awab "Open source corpus analysis tools for Malay," in In Proc. of the 5th International Conference on Language Resources and Evaluation. 2006. Citeseer.

[20] E.F. Tjong Kim Sang and F. De Meulder. "Introduction to the CoNLL-2003 shared task: Language-independent named entity recognition," in Proceedings of the seventh conference on Natural language learning at HLT-NAACL, Association for Computational Linguistics, pp.142-147, 2003

Learning from Sets of Items in Recommender Systems

Mohit Sharma
University of Minnesota, USA
Email: mohit@cs.umn.edu

F.Maxwell Harper
University of Minnesota, USA
Email: max@umn.edu

George Karypis
University of Minnesota, USA
Email: karypis@umn.edu

***Abstract*—Most of the existing recommender systems use the ratings provided by users on individual items. An alternate source of preference information is to use the ratings that users provide on sets of items. The advantages of using preferences on sets are two-fold. First, a rating provided on a set conveys some preference information about each of the set's items, which allows us to acquire a user's preferences for more items that the number of ratings that the user provided. Second, due to privacy concerns, users may not be willing to reveal their preferences on individual items explicitly but may be willing to provide a single rating on a set of items, since it provides some level of information hiding. This paper investigates two questions related to using set-level ratings in recommender system. First, how users' item-level ratings relate to their set-level ratings. Second, how collaborative filtering-based models for item-level rating prediction can take advantage of such set-level ratings. We have collected set-level ratings from active users of Movielens on sets of movies that they have rated in the past. Our analysis of these ratings shows that though the majority of the users provide the average of the ratings on a set's constituent items as the rating on the set, there exists a significant number of users that tend to consistently either under- or over-rate the sets. We have developed collaborative filtering-based methods to explicitly model these user behaviors that can be used to recommend items to users. Experiments on real data and on synthetic data that resembles the under- or over-rating behavior in the real data, demonstrate that these models can recover the overall characteristics of the underlying data and predict the user's ratings on individual items.**

Keywords–Recommender systems; Collaborative filtering; Sets or lists of items; User-behavior modeling.

I. Introduction

Recommender systems help consumers by providing suggestions that are expected to satisfy their tastes. They are successfully deployed in several domains such as e-commerce, multimedia content providers and mobile app stores. Collaborative filtering [1], [2], which takes advantage of users' past preferences to suggest relevant items, is one of the key methods used by recommender systems.

Most collaborative filtering approaches rely on past preferences provided by users on individual items. An alternate source of preferences is the user's preferences on sets of items. Example of such set-level ratings includes ratings on song playlists, music albums, reading lists, and watchlists. A rating provided by the user on a set of items conveys some information about the user's preference on each of the set's items and, as a result, it is a mechanism by which some information about user's preferences can be acquired for many items. At the same time, due to privacy concerns, users that are not willing to explicitly reveal their true preferences on individual items may provide a single rating to a set of items, since it provides some level of information hiding.

This paper investigates two questions related to using set-level preferences in recommender systems. First, how users' item-level ratings relate to the ratings that they provide on a set of items. Second, how collaborative filtering-based methods can take advantage of such set-level ratings towards making item-level rating predictions.

To answer the first question, we collected ratings on sets of movies from users of Movielens, a popular online movie recommender system [3]. Our analysis of these ratings leads to two key findings. First, for the majority of the users, the rating provided on a set can be accurately approximated by the average rating that they provided on the set's constituent items. Second, there is a considerable user population that tends to consistently either over- or under-rate the set, especially for sets that contain items on which the user's item-level ratings are diverse. Using these insights, we developed different models that can predict a user's rating on a set of items as well as on individual items. These methods solve these problems in a coupled fashion by estimating models to predict the item-level ratings and by estimating models that combine these individual ratings to derive set-level ratings.

The key contributions of the work are the following: (i) collection and analysis of a dataset that contains users' ratings both on individual items and on various sets containing these items; (ii) introduction of *Variance Offset Average Rating Model* (VOARM) to model a user's consistency to over- or under-rate the set as a function of his/her ratings on the set's constituent items; and (iii) development of collaborative filtering-based methods that take advantage of different rating models in order to estimate users' preferences on sets of items as well as on individual items.

The rest of the paper is organized as follows. Section II describes the relevant prior work. Section III describes the dataset creation process along with the analysis of the set ratings in relation to the users' ratings on their constituent items. Section IV presents the methods that we developed to estimate the item-level models from the set ratings. Section V provides information about the evaluation methodology. Section VI presents the results of the experimental evaluation. Finally, Section VII provides some concluding remarks.

II. Related Work

There has been little published work on using set-level ratings to improve the accuracy of item-level recommendations. The one exception is a recent study in which relative preference information on different groups of items was collected during a new user signup process and these preferences were then used to assign a user to a set of pre-built recommendation profiles [4]. This approach significantly reduced the time required to learn the user's preferences in order to generate recommendations for the new user. The principal difference from this approach is that in our work we try to model the user behavior that determines his/her estimated rating on a set and then use that to develop fully personalized recommendation methods that are not limited to new users.

In addition, there has been some work that has focused on recommending lists of items or bundles of items, e.g., recommendation of music playlists [5]–[7], travel packages [8]–[10], reading lists [11] and recommendation of lists under user specified budget constraints [12], [13]. However, these are not directly related to the problems explored in this paper because our focus is on learning the user's ratings on items from ratings on lists of items.

III. MOVIELENS SET RATINGS DATASET

In this section, we will present details and analysis of the ratings elicited from Movielens users on sets of movies. Additionally, we will describe the modeling of users' rating patterns on sets of movies.

A. Data collection

Movielens is a recommender system that utilizes collaborative filtering algorithms to recommend movies to their users based on their preferences. We developed a set rating widget to obtain ratings on a set of movies from the Movielens users. The set rating widget could be rated from 0.5 to 5 with a precision of 0.5. For the purpose of data collection, we selected users who were active since January 2015 and have rated at least 25 movies. The selected users were encouraged to participate by contacting them via email. The sets of movies that we asked a user to rate were created by selecting five movies at random without replacement from the movies that they have already rated. Furthermore, we limited the number of sets a user can rate in a session to 50, though users can potentially rate more sets in different sessions. The set rating widget went live on February 2016 and, for the purpose of this study, we used the set ratings that were provided until April 2016.

B. Data processing

From the initially collected data, we removed users who have rated sets within a time interval of less than one second to avoid users who might be providing the ratings at random. After this pre-processing, we were left with ratings from 854 users over 29,516 sets containing 12,549 movies. Figure 1(a) shows the distribution of the number of sets rated by the users, which shows that roughly half of the users have rated at least 45 sets in a session.

C. Analysis of the set ratings

In order to analyze how consistent a user's rating on a set is with the ratings provided by the user on the movies in the set, we computed the difference of the average of the user's ratings on the items in the set and the rating assigned by a user to the set. We will refer to this difference as *mean rating difference* (MRD). Figure 1(b) shows the distribution of the MRD values in our datasets. The majority of the sets have an MRD within a margin of 0.5 indicating that the users have rated them close to the average of their ratings on set's items. The remaining of the sets have been rated either significantly lower or higher from the average rating. We refer to these sets as the under- and the over-rated sets, respectively. Moreover, an interesting observation from the results in Figure 1(b), is that the number of under-rated sets is more than that of the over-rated sets.

In order to understand what can lead to a set being over- or under-rated, we investigated if the *diversity* of the ratings of the individual movies in a set could lead a user to under- or over-rate the set. We measured the diversity of a set as the standard deviation of the ratings that a user has provided to the individual items of the set. As shown in Figure 1(c), the sets that contain more diverse ratings (i.e., higher standard deviations) tend to get under- or over-rated more often when compared to less diverse sets. This trend was found to be statistically significant (p-value of 0.01 using t-test).

Additionally, we studied if there are users that tend to consistently over- or under-rate sets. To this end, we selected users who have rated at least 50 sets and computed the fraction of their under- and over-rated sets. We also computed the fraction of under- and over-rated sets across a random population of the same size. We generated this random population by randomly permuting the under- and over-rated sets across the users. Figures 2(a) and 2(b) show the fraction of under- and over-rated sets for both the true and random population of users, respectively. In the true population, some users tend to under- or over-rate sets significantly more than that of the random population. Using the Kolmogorov-Smirnov 2 sample test, we found this behavior of true population to be statistically different (p-value $<$ 1e-16) from that of random population.

D. Modeling users' under- and over-rating patterns

The above analysis reveals that our dataset contains users that when they are asked to assign a single rating to a set of items, some of them consistently assign a rating that is lower than the average of the ratings that they provided to the set's constituent items (they under-rate), whereas others assign a rating that is higher (they over-rate). Thus, some users are very demanding (or picky) and tend to focus on the worst items in the set, whereas other users are less demanding and tend to focus on the best items in the set.

In order to capture this user-specific *pickiness*, we investigated a model that postulates that a user rates a set by considering both the average rating of the items in the set and also the diversity of the set's items. In this model, the set's rating is determined as the sum of the average rating of the set's items and a quantity that depends on the sets diversity (e.g., the standard deviation of the set's ratings) and the user's level of pickiness. If a user is very picky, that quantity will be negative and large, resulting to the set being (severely) under-rated. On the other hand, if a user is not picky at all, that quantity will be positive and large, resulting to the set being (severely) over-rated. We will refer to this model as *Variance Offset Average Rating Model* (VOARM).

In order to determine how well this model can explain the ratings that the users in our dataset provided, we performed the following analysis. We selected the users that rated at least 20 diverse sets (their standard deviation was ≥ 0.5) and for each of these users (493 in total), we computed a user's level

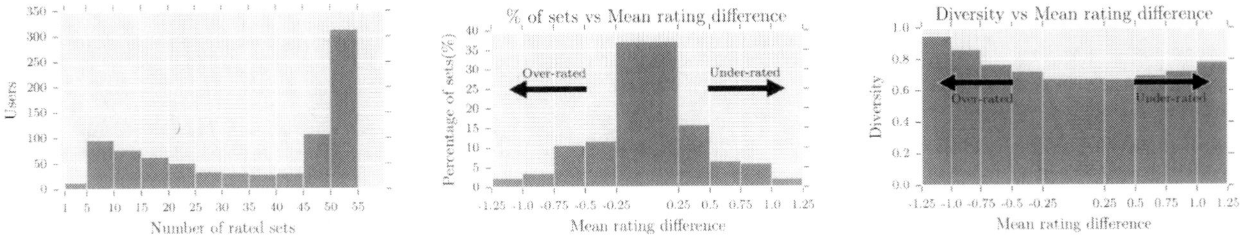

(a) (b) (c)

Figure 1. (a) The distribution of number of sets rated by the users. (b) Histogram of percentage of sets against Mean rating difference. (c) Histogram of diversity against mean rating difference.

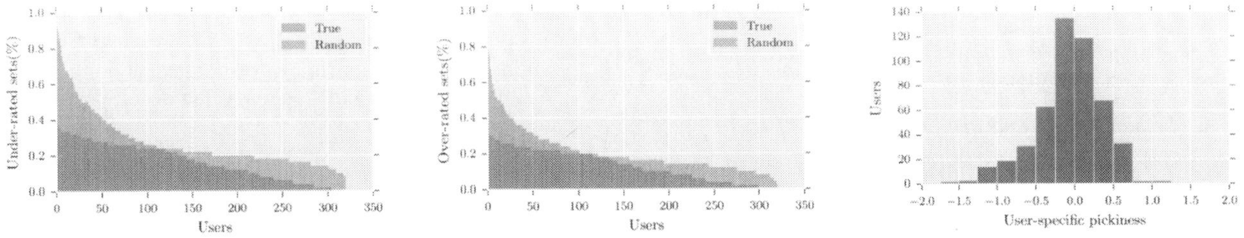

(a) (b) (c)

Figure 2. (a) Fraction of under-rated sets across users in the true and random population. (b) Fraction of over-rated sets across users in the true and random population. (c) The number of users and their computed level of pickiness.

of pickiness (β_u) as

$$\beta_u = \frac{1}{n_s} \sum_{s=1}^{n_s} \frac{r_{us} - \mu_s}{\sigma_s}, \tag{1}$$

where n_s is the number of sets rated by user u, r_{us} denotes the rating provided by user u on set $\mathcal{S}$, μ_s is the mean rating of the items in set $\mathcal{S}$ and σ_s is the standard deviation of the ratings of the items in set $\mathcal{S}$. Figure 2(c) shows the histogram of the users' level of pickiness. As can be seen from the figure, certain users tend to under- or over-rate sets with high standard deviation, and interestingly more users tend to under-rate sets than over-rate them.

We computed how well the VOARM compares against the *Average Rating Model (ARM)*, where a user rates a set as the average of the ratings that he/she gives to the set's items. The RMSE of VOARM (0.521) was found to be lower than that of the ARM (0.597), thereby suggesting that modeling users' level of pickiness could lead to better estimates.

IV. Methods

In this section, we describe various methods that use the set ratings alone or in combination with individual item ratings towards solving two problems: (i) predict a rating for a set of items, and (ii) predict a rating for individual items. Our methods solve these problems in a coupled fashion by estimating models for predicting the ratings that users will provide to the individual items and by estimating models that use these item-level ratings to derive set-level ratings.

A. Modeling users' ratings on sets

In order to estimate the preferences on individual items from the preferences on the sets, we need to make some assumptions on how a user derives a set-level rating from the ratings of the set's constituent items. Informed by our analysis of the data described in Section III, we investigated two approaches of modeling that.

Average Rating Model (ARM): This approach assumes that the rating that a user provides to a set reflects his/her average rating on all the items in the set. Specifically, if the rating of user u on set $\mathcal{S}$ is denoted by r_u^s and the size of set $\mathcal{S}$ is represented by $|\mathcal{S}|$, then the estimated rating of user u on set $\mathcal{S}$ is given by

$$\hat{r}_u^s = \frac{1}{|\mathcal{S}|} \sum_{i \in \mathcal{S}} r_{u,i}. \tag{2}$$

As the analysis in Section III showed, such a model correlates well with the actual ratings that the users provided on the majority of the sets, especially when the ratings of the constituent items are not very different.

Variance Offset Average Rating Model (VOARM): This approach is based on the VOARM method described in Section III-D. If β_u denotes the pickiness level of user u, then the estimated rating on a set is given by

$$\hat{r}_u^s = \mu_s + \beta_u \sigma_s, \tag{3}$$

where μ_s and σ_s are the mean and the standard deviation of the ratings of items in the set $\mathcal{S}$, respectively. Both μ_s and σ_s

are given by

$$\mu_s = \frac{1}{|S|}\sum_{i\in S} r_{u,i}, \quad \sigma_s = \sqrt{\frac{1}{|S|}\sum_{i\in S}(r_{u,i}-\mu_s)^2}. \tag{4}$$

B. Modeling user's ratings on items

In order to model a users' ratings on the items, similar to matrix factorization method [2], we assume that the underlying user-item rating matrix is low-rank, i.e., there is a low-dimensional latent space in which both the users and the items can be compared to each other. The rating of user u on item i can be computed as an inner product of the user and the item latent factors in that latent space. Thus, the estimated rating of user u on item i, i.e., $\hat{r}_{u,i}$, is given by

$$\hat{r}_{u,i} = \boldsymbol{p}_u^T \boldsymbol{q}_i, \tag{5}$$

where $\boldsymbol{p}_u \in \mathbb{R}^f$ is the latent representation of user u, $\boldsymbol{q}_i \in \mathbb{R}^f$ is the latent representation of item i and f is the dimensionality of the underlying latent space.

C. Combining set and item models

Our goal is to estimate the item-level ratings by learning the user and item latent factors of Equation 5; however, the ratings that we have available from the users are at the set-level. In order to use the available set-level ratings, we need to combine Equation 5 with Equations 2 and 3. To solve the problem, we assume that the actual item-level ratings used in Equations 2 and 3 correspond to the estimated ratings given by Equation 5. Hence, the estimated set-level ratings in Equations 2 and 3 are finally expressed in terms of the corresponding user and item latent factors.

D. Model learning

The parameters of the models that estimate item- and set-level ratings are the user and item latent vectors (p_u and q_i) and in the case of the VOARM method the user's pickiness level (β_u). These parameters are estimated using the user-supplied set-level ratings by minimizing a square error loss function given by

$$\mathcal{L}_{rmse}(\Theta) \equiv \sum_{u\in U}\sum_{s\in \mathcal{R}_u^s} (\hat{r}_u^s(\Theta) - r_u^s)^2, \tag{6}$$

where U represents all the users, $\mathcal{R}_u^s$ contains all the sets rated by user u, r_u^s is the original rating of user u on set $\mathcal{S}$ and $\hat{r}_u^s$ is the estimated rating of user u on set $\mathcal{S}$.

To control model complexity, we add regularization of the model parameters thereby leading to an optimization process of the following form

$$\underset{\Theta}{\text{minimize}}\, \mathcal{L}_{rmse}(\Theta) + \lambda(||\Theta||^2), \tag{7}$$

where λ is the regularization parameter. The L2-regularization is added to reduce the model complexity thereby improving its generalizability. This optimization problem can be solved by Stochastic Gradient Descent (SGD) algorithm. Also, in the VOARM method we add a fixed constant, i.e., ϵ in [0, 1], to computed σ for robustness.

If we also have ratings for the individual items, then we can incorporate these ratings into model estimation by treating each item as a set of size one.

V. Experimental Evaluation

In this section, we will describe the datasets and the evaluation methodology used to assess the proposed methods.

A. Dataset

We evaluated the proposed methods on two datasets: (i) the dataset analyzed in Section III, which will be referred to as MLRSET, and (ii) a set of synthetically generated datasets that allow us to assess how well the optimization algorithms can estimate accurate models and how their accuracy depends on various data characteristics.

The synthetic datasets were derived from the Movielens 1M dataset [14], which contains 1 million ratings from approximately 6000 users on 4000 movies. We created synthetic low-rank matrices of rank 5, 10 and 20 as follows. We started by generating two matrices $A \in \mathbb{R}^{n\times k}$ and $B \in \mathbb{R}^{m\times k}$, where n is number of users, m is number of items and $k \in [5, 10, 20]$, whose values are uniformly distributed at random in $[0, 1]$. We then computed the singular value decomposition of these matrices to obtain $A = U_A\Sigma_A V_A^T$ and $B = U_B\Sigma_B V_B^T$. We then let $P = \alpha U_A$ and $Q = \alpha U_B$ and $R = PQ^T$. Thus, the final rank k matrix R is obtained as the product of two randomly generated rank k matrices whose columns are orthogonal. Note that the parameter α was determined empirically in order to produce ratings in the range of $[-10, 10]$. We randomly selected 1000 users without replacement from the dataset and for each user we created sets containing five movies. The movies in a user's set were selected at random without replacement from the movies rated by that user. For each user, we created at least 20 and at most 50 such sets of movies. We generated VOARM-based rating for a user on a set by choosing the user's level of pickiness (the β_u parameter) at random from the range of [-2.0, 2.0]. A random $\mathcal{N}(0, 0.1)$ Gaussian noise was added to all item- and set-level ratings. For each rank, we generated 15 different synthetic datasets by varying the user-item latent factors and the users' pickiness levels.

B. Evaluation methodology

To evaluate the performance of the proposed methods we divided the available set-level ratings for each user into training, validation and test splits by randomly selecting five set-level ratings for each of the validation and test splits. The validation split was used for model selection. In order to assess the performance of the methods for item recommendations, we used a test set that contained for each user the items that were not present in the user's sets (i.e., these were absent from the training, test, and validation splits) but were present in the original user-item rating matrix used to generate the sets.

VI. Results and Discussion

The experimental evaluation of the proposed methods is done in two phases. First, we evaluated the performance of the methods using the synthetically generated datasets in order to assess how well the underlying optimization algorithms can recover the underlying data generation models and achieve good prediction performance at either the set- or item-level. Second, we evaluated the performance of the methods on the real dataset that we obtained from a subset of Movielens users (described in Section III).

TABLE I. THE AVERAGE RMSE OBTAINED BY THE PROPOSED METHODS ON SYNTHETIC DATASETS WITH RATINGS IN THE RANGE [-10, 10].

	Rank 5		Rank 10		Rank 20	
Method	Set	Item	Set	Item	Set	Item
ARM	1.206	2.949	1.498	3.545	1.619	3.880
VOARM	1.211	2.372	1.480	2.686	1.597	2.830

Underlined entries indicate the best performing scheme for each experiment.

TABLE II. THE AVERAGE RMSE OF THE PROPOSED METHODS ON SYNTHETIC DATASETS THAT CONTAIN DIVERSE SET OF ITEMS (RANK 5).

	$\sigma \geq 1$		$\sigma \geq 2$		$\sigma \geq 3$	
Method	Set	Item	Set	Item	Set	Item
ARM	1.183	3.057	1.098	3.487	1.140	4.326
VOARM	1.129	2.339	1.068	2.269	1.075	2.507

Underlined entries indicate the best performing scheme for each experiment. Each dataset was generated by keeping only the sets in which the standard deviation of the constituent item ratings (σ) is greater than or equal to the specified value.

A. *Performance on the synthetic datasets*

1) Accuracy of set- and item-level predictions: Table I shows the performance achieved by the various methods on the synthetic datasets. In these experiments, ARM acts as a baseline method and its performance relative to VOARM provides insights on the latter's ability to recover the known properties of the underlying data (that this scheme was specifically designed for). These results show that VOARM is able to achieve lower RMSE at the item-level predictions than the corresponding RMSE values obtained by ARM. However, for the set-level predictions, ARM's performance is better than VOARM's for rank 5, but for the greater ranks, i.e., 10 and 20, VOARM performs better than ARM.

In order to study how the performance of the various methods is affected by the diversity of the sets, we followed the approach described in Section V-A to generate a new set of datasets (with rank 5) in which we only kept the sets in which the standard deviation of the set's item ratings is greater than or equal to 1, 2, and 3. The RMSE results that were obtained by the different methods are shown in Table II. These results show that the performance advantage of VOARM over ARM increases with the rating diversity of the items in the sets. This is true for both the set- and item-level predictions.

The results shown in Tables I and II indicate that VOARM is able to recover the known underlying characteristics of the dataset and consequently lead to better prediction performance. To further illustrate this, Figure 3 plots the actual vs estimated weights that model a user's level of pickiness in VOARM (i.e., β_u parameters), which shows that VOARM is able to recover the overall characteristics of the underlying data.

2) Effect of adding item-level ratings: In most real-world scenarios, in addition to set-level ratings, we will also have available ratings on individual items as well, e.g., users may provide ratings on music albums and as well as on tracks in the albums. Also, there may exist some users that are not concerned about keeping their item-level ratings private. To assess how well VOARM can take advantage of such item-level ratings we performed two sets of experiments. In the first experiment, we added in the synthetic datasets a set of item-level ratings for the same set of users for which we have set-level ratings. The number of item-level ratings was kept to 35% of their set-level ratings and the items that were added were disjoint from those that were part of the sets that they rated. Additionally, we used the matrix factorization (MF) method to estimate the user and item latent factors without any set-level ratings by utilizing only the added item-level ratings. In the second experiment, we selected 500 additional users (beyond those that exist in the synthetically generated datasets) and added a random subset of 60 ratings per user from the items that belong to the existing users' sets.

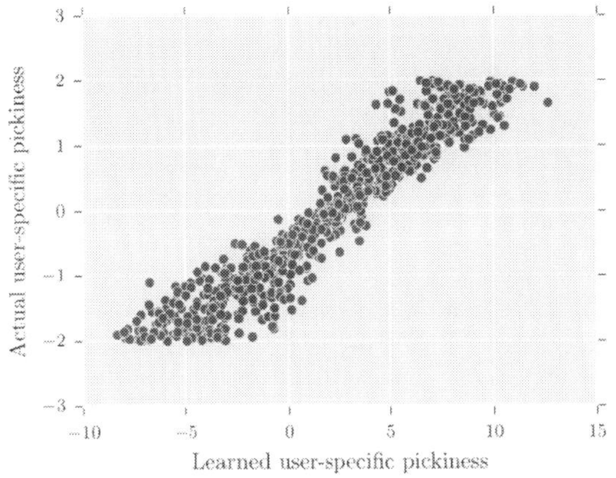

Figure 3. A scatter plot of the estimated and actual parameters that model a user's level of pickiness in VOARM (Rank 5).

TABLE III. AVERAGE RMSE PERFORMANCE OF VOARM WHEN USING ADDITIONAL ITEM-LEVEL RATINGS FROM THE SAME USERS OR A DIFFERENT SET OF USERS (RANK 5).

	set only	+items	+users
Set	1.211	1.190	0.447
Item	2.372	2.169	0.757
MF	—	2.373	—

The entries marked with "—" correspond to combinations that are not applicable.

The performance that was achieved by VOARM on these datasets along with the performance in the original set-only dataset is shown in Table III. The "set only" columns show the results of the models that were estimated using only set-level ratings. The "+items" columns show the results of the models that were estimated using the sets of "set only" and also some additional ratings on a different set of items from the same users that provided the set-level ratings. The "+users" columns show the results of the models that were estimated using the sets of "set only" and item-level ratings of a different set of users. We also show the item-level RMSE of the MF models estimated using only the additional item-level ratings from the same users that provided set-level ratings. These results show that by adding these additional item-level ratings

TABLE IV. THE RMSE PERFORMANCE OF THE PROPOSED METHODS ON MLRSET DATASET.

	ARM			VOARM		
	set only	+items	+users	set only	+items	+users
Set	0.633	0.633	0.605	0.632	0.632	0.618
Item	1.082	0.972	0.866	1.005	0.966	0.894
MF	—	1.077	—	—	1.077	—

The meaning of these columns is same as that of Table III.

VOARM's performance improves considerably. Also, VOARM outperforms MF for the task of item-level rating prediction when additional item-level ratings are available for the users. Furthermore, it is promising that when item-level ratings is available for another set of users, the prediction performance for those users for which only set-level ratings is available also improves considerably. Hence, using both item- and set-level ratings can lead to better item recommendations for the users.

B. *Performance on the Movielens-based real dataset*

Our final experiment used the two different methods (ARM and VOARM) to estimate both set- and item-level rating prediction models using the real set-level rating dataset that we obtained from Movielens users. In addition, we assessed how well the proposed methods can take advantage of additional item-level ratings. In the first experiment, we added 20% of the users' set-level ratings as additional item-level ratings and the items that were added were disjoint from those that were part of the sets that they rated. In the second experiment, we added ratings from 500 additional users (beyond those that have participated in the survey), and these users have provided on an average 20,000 ratings for the items that belong to the existing users' sets. The results of these experiments are shown in Table IV.

In the case when we have only set-level ratings, for prediction of item-level ratings, VOARM achieves lower RMSE than ARM. In terms of the accuracy of the set-level predictions, similar to the trends that we observed in the earlier experiments, VOARM does somewhat better than ARM.

For the experiments that include both set- and item-level ratings from the same set of users, we see that performance of both methods improves for item-level predictions. Moreover, VOARM outperforms not only ARM but also MF for item-level predictions. Finally, for the experiments that include set-level ratings of a set of users and item-level ratings from a disjoint set of users we see a significant improvement in performance for both the set- and item-level predictions.

Similar to our results on synthetic datasets, it is promising that the item-level ratings from additional users have significantly improved the performance for the users who have provided only the set-level ratings. The overall consistency of the results between the synthetically generated and the real dataset suggests that VOARM is able to capture the tendency that some users have to consistently under- or over-rate diverse sets of items.

VII. CONCLUSION

In this work, we studied how users' ratings on sets of items relate to their ratings on the sets' individual items. We collected ratings from active users of Movielens on sets of movies and based on our analysis we developed collaborative filtering-based models that try to explicitly model the users' behavior in providing the ratings on sets of items. Through extensive experiments on synthetic and real data, we showed that the proposed methods can model the users' behavior as seen in the real data and predict the users' ratings on individual items.

For future work, we plan to study how the performance of the proposed approaches varies with the different number of items in sets. Furthermore, it will be interesting to investigate if, similar to the diversity of ratings in sets, there exist other properties at item-level or set-level that can affect a user's ratings on sets of items.

REFERENCES

[1] B. Sarwar, G. Karypis, J. Konstan, and J. Riedl, "Item-based collaborative filtering recommendation algorithms," in Proceedings of the 10th international conference on World Wide Web. ACM, 2001, pp. 285–295.

[2] Y. Koren, R. Bell, C. Volinsky et al., "Matrix factorization techniques for recommender systems," Computer, vol. 42, no. 8, 2009, pp. 30–37.

[3] "Movielens recommender system," 2017, URL: http://www.movielens.org/ [accessed: 2017-02-26].

[4] S. Chang, F. M. Harper, and L. Terveen, "Using groups of items for preference elicitation in recommender systems," in Proceedings of the 18th ACM Conference on Computer Supported Cooperative Work & Social Computing, ser. CSCW '15. New York, NY, USA: ACM, 2015, pp. 1258–1269. [Online]. Available: http://doi.acm.org/10.1145/2675133.2675210

[5] S. Chen, J. L. Moore, D. Turnbull, and T. Joachims, "Playlist prediction via metric embedding," in Proceedings of the 18th ACM SIGKDD International Conference on Knowledge Discovery and Data Mining, ser. KDD '12. New York, NY, USA: ACM, 2012, pp. 714–722. [Online]. Available: http://doi.acm.org/10.1145/2339530.2339643

[6] N. Aizenberg, Y. Koren, and O. Somekh, "Build your own music recommender by modeling internet radio streams," in Proceedings of the 21st international conference on World Wide Web. ACM, 2012, pp. 1–10.

[7] J. L. Moore, S. Chen, T. Joachims, and D. Turnbull, "Learning to embed songs and tags for playlist prediction." in ISMIR, 2012, pp. 349–354.

[8] R. Interdonato, S. Romeo, A. Tagarelli, and G. Karypis, "A versatile graph-based approach to package recommendation," in 2013 IEEE 25th International Conference On Tools with Artificial Intelligence. IEEE, 2013, pp. 857–864.

[9] Q. Liu, E. Chen, H. Xiong, Y. Ge, Z. Li, and X. Wu, "A cocktail approach for travel package recommendation," IEEE Transactions on Knowledge and Data Engineering, vol. 26, no. 2, Feb 2014, pp. 278–293.

[10] M. Xie, L. V. Lakshmanan, and P. T. Wood, "Comprec-trip: A composite recommendation system for travel planning," in Data Engineering (ICDE), 2011 IEEE 27th International Conference on. IEEE, 2011, pp. 1352–1355.

[11] Y. Liu, M. Xie, and L. V. Lakshmanan, "Recommending user generated item lists," in Proceedings of the 8th ACM Conference on Recommender Systems, ser. RecSys '14. New York, NY, USA: ACM, 2014, pp. 185–192. [Online]. Available: http://doi.acm.org/10.1145/2645710.2645750

[12] M. Xie, L. V. Lakshmanan, and P. T. Wood, "Breaking out of the box of recommendations: from items to packages," in Proceedings of the fourth ACM conference on Recommender systems. ACM, 2010, pp. 151–158.

[13] I. Benouaret and D. Lenne, "A package recommendation framework for trip planning activities," in Proceedings of the 10th ACM Conference on Recommender Systems, ser. RecSys '16. New York, NY, USA: ACM, 2016, pp. 203–206. [Online]. Available: http://doi.acm.org/10.1145/2959100.2959183

[14] "Movielens 1M dataset," 2017, URL: https://grouplens.org/datasets/movielens/1m [accessed: 2017-02-26].

Item-Based Explanations for User-Based Recommendations

Marius Kaminskas
Frederico Durão
and Derek Bridge
Department of Computer Science
Insight Centre for Data Analytics
University College Cork
Ireland
Email: marius.kaminskas|fred.durao|derek.bridge@insight-centre.org

***Abstract*—Explanations can increase user satisfaction with recommender systems. While it is relatively easy to explain the recommendations of a content-based or an item-based collaborative recommender system, user-based collaborative recommendations are harder to explain. In this work, we adopt an approach from the literature that generates *explanation rules* for user-based collaborative-filtering recommendations. These rules are item-based: for example, "If you liked *Toy Story* then you might also like *Finding Nemo*". We modify the approach by proposing two new, alternative measures of explanation rule quality. We evaluate the two new measures in a user study and show that users prefer explanation rules whose antecedents are both accurate and unique with respect to the recommended item.**

Keywords–Recommender systems; Explanations; Collaborative filtering.

I. INTRODUCTION

An explanation of a recommendation is any content, additional to the recommendation itself, that is presented to the user with the goal of increasing (among other things) transparency, trust in the system, and decision-making effectiveness [1]. The problem that we examine in this work is how to produce effective explanations (ones that help the user make a good decision) for recommendations made by user-based collaborative filtering (CF) recommender systems.

User-based CF recommender systems were among the first recommenders, and they remain important, e.g., as part of larger ensembles of recommenders. They find the active user's nearest-neighbours and use the neighbours' ratings to predict the active user's rating for items that are in the neighbours' profiles but not in the active user's profile. It is relatively easy to explain the recommendations of content-based recommenders, e.g., by displaying meta-descriptions (such as features or tags) that the active user's profile and the recommended item have in common [1]. Item-based CF recommendations are also amenable to explanation, e.g., by displaying items in the user's profile that are similar to the recommended item [2]. User-based CF recommendations, on the other hand, are harder to explain. Displaying the identities of the active user's neighbours is unlikely to be effective (and may not be ethical) because, when these systems are deployed at scale, the user will not know the neighbours; displaying their profiles is unlikely to be effective too, since even the parts of their profiles they have in common with the active user will be too large to be readily comprehended.

This paper adopts the approach of Bridge & Dunleavy [3], who proposed an explanation generation algorithm for user-based CF recommendations. The algorithm produces explanations in the form of *explanation rules*: for example, "If you liked *Toy Story* then you might also like *Finding Nemo*". The antecedent of an explanation rule (in this case, *Toy Story*) characterizes a subset of the active user's tastes that are predictive of the recommended item, which appears in the consequent of the rule (in this case *Finding Nemo*). In this paper, we refer to such explanations as being in an *item-based style* [4]. They are a familiar style of explanation, since they are used by amazon.com [2].

However, the Bridge & Dunleavy algorithm has a popularity bias (see next section). For this reason, in this paper we propose two new, alternative measures of explanation rule quality that can be used in the algorithm's objective function. The remainder of the paper is structured as follows: Section II describes Bridge & Dunleavy's rule generation algorithm. Section III proposes two new, alternative measures of quality for use in the algorithm. Section IV extends the way in which candidate opinions are obtained from neighbours' profiles. Section V presents both offline experiments and a user study. Section VI reviews related work.

II. GENERATING EXPLANATION RULES

The algorithm for generating explanation rules presented in [3] constructs explanations in a way that is similar to the mining of association rules (ARs) [5]. Unlike in AR mining, the literals constituting explanation rules represent *item opinions* rather than just the items. Given a set of items I, an item opinion is represented by a tuple $(i, opinion)$, such that $i \in I$ and $opinion \in \{dislike, neutral, like\}$. We will often write just i in place of $(i, opinion)$ allowing context to make clear which is intended. Since most CF datasets contain item ratings on a $1-5$ scale, Bridge & Dunleavy convert the numerical ratings into opinions using a rating threshold, with items rated lower than 3.0 considered *disliked* by a user, items rated as 3.0 assigned a *neutral* opinion, and items rated higher than 3.0 considered *liked*.

Having discretized item ratings into item opinions, an explanation rule R for a user u and a recommended item y is built to contain a *set* of item opinions in its antecedent and a *single* (positive) opinion of the recommended item y in its

Data: user profiles U, active user u, recommended item y, explanation partner v
Result: an explanation rule for y

$R \leftarrow$ if _ then $(y, like)$;
$Cs \leftarrow candidates(u, v)$;
while $Cs \neq \{\}$ **do**
  $Rs \leftarrow$ the set of all new rules formed by adding singly each candidate opinion in Cs to the antecedent of R;
  $R^* \leftarrow \arg\max_{R^* \in Rs} f_{obj}(R^*)$;
  if $f_{obj}(R^*) \leq f_{obj}(R)$ **then**
    return R;
  $R \leftarrow R^*$;
  Remove from Cs the candidate opinion that was used to create R;
end
return R;

Figure 1. Creating an explanation rule

consequent: $R : X \Rightarrow (y, like)$, where $X = \{(i, opinion) : i \in I \setminus y\}$.

Rule generation is based on identifying an *explanation partner* – the most similar neighbour of the active user u who rated the recommended item positively. Subsequently, the explanation rule is built from the item opinions *shared* by the active user and the explanation partner. Items for which the active user u and the explanation partner v share the same opinion are called *candidate opinions*:

$$candidates(u, v) = \{(i, opin) : (i, opin) \in profile_u \wedge (i, opin) \in profile_v\} \quad (1)$$

where, e.g., $profile_u$ is the set of all of user u's item opinions.

Having identified the set of candidate opinions, the rule's antecedent is constructed in a greedy fashion — at each iteration, the candidate opinion which maximizes an objective function is added to the antecedent (see Figure 1).

Bridge & Dunleavy used *accuracy* as the objective function f_{obj}:

$$acc(X \Rightarrow y) = \frac{|\{u \in U : X \subset profile_u \wedge y \in profile_u\}|}{|\{u \in U : X \subset profile_u\}|} \quad (2)$$

where U is the set of all users. A rule's accuracy is equivalent to the *confidence* metric used in AR mining [6].

Bridge & Dunleavy resolved ties (equally accurate rules) using *coverage*, defined as the probability of observing the antecedent of the rule in a user's profile (equivalent to the *support* metric in AR mining):

$$cov(X \Rightarrow y) = \frac{|\{u \in U : X \subseteq profile_u\}|}{|U|} \quad (3)$$

In this work, we extend Bridge & Dunleavy's approach with two contributions. First, we observe that the objective function f_{obj} can be implemented using measures other than accuracy and coverage. We propose and evaluate two new, alternative measures. Second, we extend the candidate opinions from those of a *single* explanation partner to those of a *set* of the active user's neighbours. In the next two sections we describe the two contributions in greater detail.

III. Proposed Rule Utility Metrics

While accuracy and coverage offer an intuitive way of measuring the strength of the explanation rules, they are biased toward popular items. For instance, the movie *Star Wars* is frequently rated and therefore co-occurs in user profiles with many other (not necessarily related) movies. Relying on accuracy and coverage may lead to explanations that are trivial or irrelevant with respect to the recommended item, e.g., "If you liked *Star Wars* then you might like *Fargo*".

Intuitively, an item opinion in an explanation rule is good the more it is *unique* with respect to the recommended item. In other words, we are looking for measures that promote antecedent items that are accurate (i.e., result in high accuracy) with respect to the consequent item, but also penalize antecedent items that achieve high accuracy with (many) other consequent items.

Within AR mining, there has similarly been a quest for measures of AR interestingness, beyond confidence and support, including measures of *lift* and *conviction* [6]. However, these measures in general try to counter-act the tendency of the accuracy measure to favour rules with popular *consequents*. Hence, these measures do not achieve what we want to achieve. In our case, the consequent is a given: it is the item recommended by the user-based CF system. Our goal is to build explanation rules using measures that counter-act the tendency of the accuracy measure to favour popular items in *antecedents*.

To the best of our knowledge, the uniqueness property that we seek does not correspond to any of the existing measures of AR interestingness. We experimented with a number of these existing measures and others, such as selecting a rule whose antecedents were similar to its consequent. But none of these resulted in the selection of distinctive ('unique') antecedents. We therefore propose two new, alternative measures — one that discounts a rule's accuracy by the antecedent's popularity and the other that discounts its accuracy by the antecedent's explanatory power.

A. Popularity-discounted accuracy

Our *popularity-discounted accuracy* (pda) measure is designed to balance the accuracy of a rule and the popularity of its antecedent. Specifically, we discount the rule's accuracy by the number of items that could potentially be explained by the antecedent, i.e., the number of items in the dataset (other than the recommended item) that co-occur with the antecedent in at least one user's profile:

$$pda(X \Rightarrow y) = \frac{acc(X \Rightarrow y)}{|\{j \in I \setminus X \cup \{y\} : \exists u \in U, X \subset profile_u \wedge j \in profile_u\}| + 1} \quad (4)$$

Initial analysis of explanations generated using pda as the objective function in Figure 1 revealed that the explanation rules tended to contain more items in their antecedents compared to the original approach (which, for two datasets, was reported to contain no more than 3 items in the antecedent [3]). Therefore, to restrict the lengths of the rules, we included an additional constraint in the algorithm: the rule R is returned if either $f_{obj}(R^*) \leq f_{obj}(R)$ *or* if $acc(R^*) \leq acc(R)$; see Figure 2. This additional constraint ensures the quality of the rules and restricts their lengths so that they are closer to those of the original approach.

B. Uniqueness-discounted accuracy

Our *uniqueness-discounted accuracy* (uda) metric is similar to the popularity-discounted accuracy, but instead of counting the number of *all* potential explanations that could be generated from the antecedent, it counts the items that the antecedent can explain *better* (i.e., with a higher accuracy) than the target item y:

$$uda(X \Rightarrow y) = \frac{acc(X \Rightarrow y)}{|\{j \in I \setminus X \cup \{y\} : acc(X \Rightarrow j) > acc(X \Rightarrow y)\}| + 1} \quad (5)$$

Again we included the additional constraint on the rule's accuracy in the algorithm to avoid generating longer rules.

IV. Extended Candidate Opinions

In Figure 1, the candidate opinions (the set Cs) are taken from the profile of a *single explanation partner* — the most similar neighbour of the active user who liked the recommended item. However, user-based CF recommender systems generate item predictions using a larger number of nearest-neighbours.

To reflect this in the explanation generation process, we evaluate a variant of the algorithm where the candidate opinions are obtained from the profiles of *all* the active user's nearest-neighbours (where the size of this set is given by the underlying user-based CF recommender system).

In recommendation, the contribution of a neighbour to item predictions is weighted by the neighbour's similarity to the active user. We mirror this in the revised explanation generation algorithm by weighting each candidate opinion by the neighbour's similarity:

$$R^* \leftarrow \arg \max_{R^* \in Rs} f_{obj}(R^*) \cdot sim(u, v) \quad (6)$$

where u is the active user and v is the neighbour whose profile contains the candidate opinion used to obtain R^*. If the candidate opinion is contained in more than one neighbours' profiles, the highest $sim(u, v)$ is used.

The changes that we have proposed in this section and the previous one are summarized in Figure 2.

Data: user profiles U, active user u, recommended item y, nearest neighbours NN
Result: an explanation rule for y

$R \leftarrow$ if _ then $(y, like)$;
$Cs \leftarrow \bigcup_{v \in NN} candidates(u, v)$;
while $Cs \neq \{\}$ **do**
  $Rs \leftarrow$ the set of all new rules formed by adding singly each candidate opinion in Cs to the antecedent of R;
  $R^* \leftarrow \arg \max_{R^* \in Rs} f_{obj}(R^*) \cdot sim(u, v)$;
  if $f_{obj}(R^*) \leq f_{obj}(R) \vee acc(R^*) \leq acc(R)$ **then**
    return R;
  $R \leftarrow R^*$;
  Remove from Cs the candidate opinion that was used to create R;
end
return R;

Figure 2. Creating an explanation rule: revised

V. Experiments

Our main goal is to compare the effectiveness of the two new measures (pda and uda) against the original accuracy-based approach (acc). Each measure can be used by taking candidate opinions either from a single explanation partner (designated ep) or from the set of neighbours (designated nn), as in Section IV, resulting in a total of six alternatives: acc+ep, pda+ep, uda+ep, acc+nn, pda+nn and uda+nn.

For extended candidate opinions, all experiments were conducted using a neighbourhood of 150 users. Furthermore, in all experiments, we used only the positive item opinions as candidates for rule generation (i.e., opinions of the form $(i, like)$). The positive opinions were identified by selecting items having a rating higher than 3.0. We leave the exploration of alternative rating thresholds and the possible use of negative and neutral item opinions for future work.

Explanation rules can only be evaluated using feedback from real users, since, to the best of our knowledge, there are no offline metrics that can quantify the "goodness" of an explanation. However, comparing six alternatives in a user study would result in a high cognitive load for the participants. Therefore, as a first step in the evaluation procedure, we performed offline experiments in an effort to reduce the number of approaches to be evaluated in a user study.

A. Offline experiments

In the offline experiments, we used the MovieLens 1M dataset [7]. For each user, we split her rating data into train and test items. Then, we randomly selected one highly rated item (i.e., an item with a rating of 5.0) for explanation generation. (In other words, we are explaining an item that we know the user likes.) The evaluation was performed using a 5-fold cross-validation, where each fold contains 20% of user ratings as a test set. The same set of test items was used to evaluate the six different approaches.

The quality of the explanation rules was measured using a number of metrics all of which provide a single value per-rule. Those metrics that are defined at the level of individual items (i.e., novelty and similarity) were aggregated into a rule-level score using three different strategies — taking the minimum, maximum, and average value as the rule score. The full set of metrics is as follows:

- The *overlap* with the original accuracy-based algorithm. The overlap value is computed as the number of antecedent items in the generated rule that are also present in the original (accuracy-based) version of the same rule, normalized by the length of the evaluated rule;
- The *accuracy* and *coverage* metrics (see 2,3);

- The *rule length*, defined as the number of item opinions in the rule's antecedent;
- The minimum, maximum, and average *novelty* of the items in the rule's antecedent, where the novelty of item i is $-log_2 P(i)$ where $P(i) = |\{u : i \in profile_u\}|/|U|$, and U is the set of all users in the dataset;
- The minimum, maximum, and average *similarity* of the items in the rule's antecedent to the item in the consequent, where $similarity(i, y) = \frac{|L_i \cap L_y|}{|L_i \cup L_y|}$ and L_i and L_y are sets of text labels describing items i and y respectively. In addition to the movie descriptors included in the MovieLens dataset (a vocabulary of 18 genres, 1.65 genres per movie on average), we scraped IMDb plot keywords for each movie and kept those labels that appeared in the profiles of at least 10 movies. This resulted in an average of 60 labels per movie.

The metrics were computed for each explanation rule and then averaged over all test cases.

We recognise that these evaluation metrics are mere proxies for what we regard as good explanations, but we believe that they can nevertheless help us to reduce the six alternatives down to a few for use in a user study.

B. Results of offline experiments

The results are shown in Figure 3, which shows the metrics computed over approximately 27,600 data points (across the 5 cross-validation folds).

The lengths of the rules for all approaches is below 4 on average. But there are rules that are longer than those reported by Bridge & Dunleavy: they reported a maximum length of 3 [3], but the difference may be because they used a different version of the dataset (MovieLens 100k), as well as the other changes described in earlier parts of this paper.

Our results indicate that, *pda+ep* and *uda+ep*, which use a single explanation partner, produce rules similar to the original *acc+ep* (an average overlap of 75%). The average overlap between *pda+ep* and *uda+ep* themselves (not shown in the figure), is 59%. Methods that use extended candidate opinions (*acc+nn*, *pda+nn* and *uda+nn*) have a smaller overlap with the original *acc+ep* and also with each other (an average of 50% between *acc+nn* and each of *pda+nn* and *uda+nn*).

Rules computed from extended candidate opinions (*nn* approaches) achieve higher average accuracy, but lower coverage compared to the approaches that use a single explanation partner (*ep*). The larger set of candidate opinions from which to choose allows the algorithms to identify item opinion patterns that are more accurate but less frequent and therefore potentially more interesting to the user.

The *pda* approaches produce rules with the highest novelty. This is not surprising, since *pda* favours rules with less popular items. Also, as expected, the extended candidate opinions approaches (*nn*) tend to generate rules with more novel items. The two combined, *pda+nn*, gives highest novelty.

With regard to rule antecedent similarity to the recommended item, extended candidate opinion approaches (*nn*) achieve a slightly higher similarity compared to the single explanation partner approaches (*ep*).

Overall, the higher accuracy and novelty achieved by the *nn* approaches lead us to believe that the use of extended candidate opinions is beneficial for the rule generation and we focus our user study on *acc+nn*, *pda+nn* and *uda+nn*.

C. User study

The three explanation generation approaches identified as the most promising during the offline evaluation stage were subsequently compared in a user study. For this user study, we employed the 10M version of the MovieLens dataset, rather than the 1M version used in the offline experiments, since it contains movies that are more recent, which are more likely to be recognized by the study participants [7]. To further increase the chances of user familiarity with the recommended item, we filtered the test sets (below) to include only movies produced in the year 2000 or later and having at least 100 ratings in the training set. It is important to note that we only applied the filtering to test sets, not the items appearing in antecedents of explanation rules.

Each user's item ratings were split into a train set (80%), from which antecedents can be picked, and a test set (20%), which was filtered (above) and from which one highly-rated test item (i.e., an item which we know the user likes) was picked and treated as the item to be recommended to the user. We did this for each of 100 randomly-chosen users, giving us 100 recommendations. For each recommendation, we generated three explanation rules (*acc+nn*, *pda+nn* and *uda+nn*). If the antecedents of the three explanation rules did not differ pairwise by at least one item, then we picked a different highly-rated item from the test set and generated its explanations. This ensures that we have no redundant survey questions, where participants are asked to judge identical explanations.

The 100 recommendations (each with three explanation rules) were partitioned across 5 questionnaires, containing 20 recommendations each. For each of the 20 recommendations, the questionnaires showed the recommended movie and the three explanation rules. The order in which the explanation rules were displayed was determined at random, e.g., sometimes *acc+nn* was the first of the three, sometimes the second and sometimes the last. The questionnaire asked participants to mark all explanations that they found helpful in choosing the movie recommendation. If they did not know the recommended movie or if unknown movies in the explanations prevented them from making a fair comparison, they were asked to mark an explicit option ("None of the explanations are helpful"). Hence, for each recommendation, participants can mark zero, one, two or three of the explanations as helpful.

From July to September of 2016, 50 volunteers (mostly students and researchers from Ireland and Brazil) took part in the study. Each participant responded to exactly one questionnaire through a dedicated web site, 10 volunteers per questionnaire. In order to help participants, all questionnaires had introductory guidelines for the experiment and links to synopses of the movies. The participants were also free to gather more information about the movies from any source of their choice, such as YouTube or IMDb.

D. Results of user study

Table I summarizes the responses. The maximum possible in each cell is 200: for each of the 20 recommendations up to

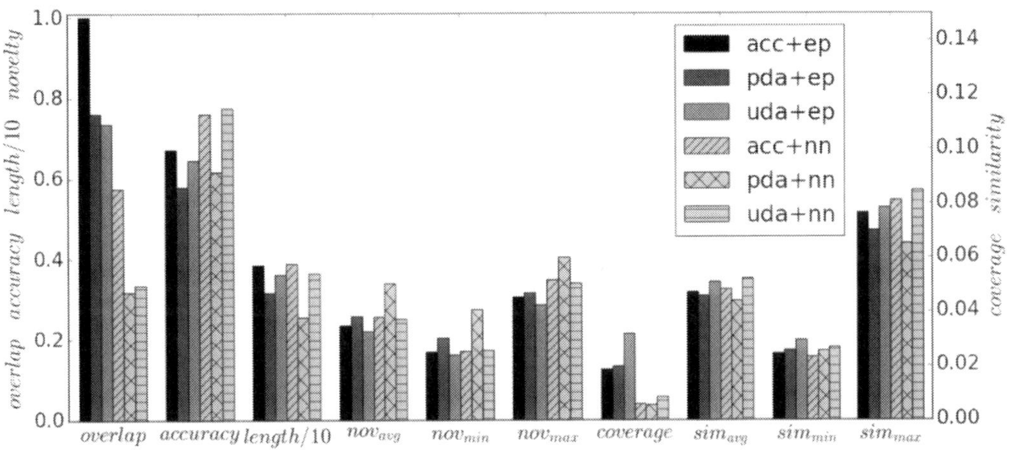

Figure 3. Offline experiments: results

TABLE I. USER STUDY: RESULTS

	Q1	Q2	Q3	Q4	Q5	Total
acc+nn	67	58	57	66	82	330
pda+nn	69	57	43	55	71	295
uda+nn	72	85	95	80	101	433
None	45	63	50	49	24	231

10 people could have found them helpful. Hence the maximum possible across the questionnaires (Q1 to Q5) is 1000.

As can be seen, *uda+nn* produced by far the most helpful explanations. Our other new measure, *pda*, was not successful: *pda+nn* produced the least helpful explanations. In particular, *uda+nn* explanations were selected 1.3 more times than *acc+nn* and nearly 1.5 more times than *pda+nn*. Using 99% level two-tailed Student's t-tests, we observed that, in this study, i) *acc+nn* and *pda+nn* are not statistically different (p-value = 0.333); ii) *acc+nn* and *uda+nn* are statistically different (p-value = 0.017); and iii) *pda+nn* and *uda+nn* are statistically different (p-value = 0.005). From this, we conclude it is not statistically correct to claim that *acc+nn* is superior to *pda+nn*, but *uda+nn* is superior to both.

VI. RELATED WORK

Several papers consider the role of explanations in recommender systems. They agree that providing explanations can lead to greater user satisfaction and to acceptance of a recommended item. Justifying why an item is recommended is often welcomed by users [1] [8] [9]. Herlocker et al. report that the benefits include education, acceptance, user involvement and justification [8]. In a similar fashion, Tintarev & Masthoff outline six motivations for explanations in recommender systems: transparency, trust, scrutability, effectiveness and efficiency, persuasiveness and satisfaction [9].

Vig et al. [4] divide explanations into three main kinds: user-based (such as showing the user a histogram of their neighbours' ratings, e.g., [8]) item-based (as used in this paper and in amazon.com [2]), and feature-based (such as using attribute-value pairs [10], item content (e.g., from news items) [11], user-generated tags [4] [12], or features and opinions mined from user reviews [13] [14]). Some systems combine the different types of explanations; for example, Symeonidis et al. combine feature-based with item-based [15].

Herlocker et al. conducted a user survey to test the persuasiveness of twenty-one different styles of user-based and feature-based explanation [8]. Similarly, Gedikli et al.'s study tested, among other things, the efficiency and effectiveness of ten different styles of explanation [12]: seven of them drawn from [8], plus a user-based pie-chart and two new forms of feature-based explanation using user-generated tags. For Herlocker et al., histograms of user ratings were the most persuasive; Gedikli et al. found their tag explanations to most increase satisfaction. Neither study included explanations in the item-based style.

Bilgic & Mooney ran a user study to compare item-based explanations (which they refer to as *influence-style explanations*) with user-based and feature-based explanations [16]. In their study, a user is shown a recommendation with an explanation, and she is asked to rate the item before and after consumption. Bilgic & Mooney found that user-based explanations cause users to over-estimate the quality of items; the other two forms of explanation were found to result in significantly more accurate estimations of final ratings.

One issue that is often ignored is the transparency [1] or fidelity [3] of the explanation, i.e., the extent to which the explanation reveals the logic of the recommender. (Gedikli et al. refer to this as *objective transparency* to contrast it with *perceived transparency*, i.e., whether the user thinks that the logic has been revealed [12].) A lot of the work in this area is characterized by explanations that are divorced from the recommender. By contrast, we believe that one advantage of the Bridge & Dunleavy scheme that we have adopted in this paper is that it does have some fidelity to the operation of the underlying user-based CF recommender: both the recommendations and the explanations are based on opinions shared by the active user and her nearest-neighbours.

VII. CONCLUSION

We have built on the work of Bridge & Dunleavy, which generates explanation rules in the item-based style for items recommended by user-based CF recommender systems [3]. In particular, we have proposed two new, alternative measures of explanation rule quality for use in the algorithm's objective function, *pda* and *uda*. These new measures attempt to overcome the tendency of the original accuracy and coverage measure to favour popular items. We also proposed extending the set of candidate opinions from which explanation rule antecedents are constructed: instead of using opinions from a single explanation partner, we modify the algorithm to allow it to use opinions from the active user's nearest neighbours.

We evaluated our proposed modifications in both an offline experiment and a user study. The offline experiment indicated the benefits of using the extended set of candidate opinions (from the nearest neighbours), resulting in rules that are both more accurate and contain more items that are novel. The online study showed that users found that explanation rules which were generated using the *uda* measure were far more helpful than those produced using *pda* and Bridge & Dunleavy's accuracy and coverage measure.

ACKNOWLEDGMENTS

This publication has emanated from research conducted with the financial support of Science Foundation Ireland (SFI) under Grant Number SFI/12/RC/2289. The work has also been supported by the Department of Computer Science, Federal University of Bahia, Brazil.

REFERENCES

[1] N. Tintarev and J. Masthoff, "Explaining recommendations: Design and evaluation," in Recommender Systems Handbook, F. Ricci, L. Rokach, and B. Shapira, Eds. Springer, 2015, pp. 353–382.

[2] G. Linden, B. Smith, and J. York, "Amazon.com recommendations: Item-to-item collaborative filtering," IEEE Internet Computing, vol. 7, no. 1, 2003, pp. 76–80.

[3] D. Bridge and K. Dunleavy, "If you liked Herlocker et al.'s explanations paper, then you might like this paper too," in Procs. of the Joint Workshop on Interfaces and Human Decision Making for Recommender Systems (Worskhop Programme of the Eighth ACM Conference on Recommender Systems). CEUR-WS.org, vol.1253, 2014, pp. 22–27.

[4] J. Vig, S. Sen, and J. Riedl, "Tagsplanations: Explaining recommendations using tags," in Procs. of the 14th International Conference on Intelligent User Interfaces. ACM, 2009, pp. 47–56.

[5] J. J. Sandvig, B. Mobasher, and R. Burke, "Robustness of collaborative recommendation based on association rule mining," in Procs. of the ACM Conference on Recommender Systems. ACM, 2007, pp. 105–112.

[6] L. Geng and H. J. Hamilton, "Interestingness measures for data mining: A survey," ACM Comput. Surv., vol. 38, no. 3, 2006, pp. 9:1–9:32.

[7] F. M. Harper and J. A. Konstan, "The MovieLens Datasets: History and Context," ACM Trans. Interact. Intell. Syst., vol. 5, no. 4, Dec. 2015, pp. 19:1–19:19. [Online]. Available: http://doi.acm.org/10.1145/2827872

[8] J. L. Herlocker, J. A. Konstan, and J. Riedl, "Explaining collaborative filtering recommendations," in Procs. of the ACM Conference on Computer Supported Cooperative Work. ACM, 2000, pp. 241–250.

[9] N. Tintarev and J. Masthoff, "Effective explanations of recommendations: User-centered design," in Procs. of the ACM Conference on Recommender Systems. ACM, 2007, pp. 153–156.

[10] C. Scheel, A. Castellanos, T. Lee, and E. W. De Luca, "The reason why: A survey of explanations for recommender systems," in Adaptive Multimedia Retrieval: Semantics, Context, and Adaptation, A. Nürnberger, S. Stober, B. Larsen, and M. Detyniecki, Eds. Springer, 2014, pp. 67–84.

[11] R. Blanco, D. Ceccarelli, C. Lucchese, R. Perego, and F. Silvestri, "You Should Read This! Let Me Explain You Why: Explaining News Recommendations to Users," in Procs. of the Twenty-first ACM International Conference on Information and Knowledge Management. ACM, 2012, pp. 1995–1999.

[12] F. Gedikli, D. Jannach, and M. Ge, "How should I epxlain? A comparison of different explanation types for recommender systems," Int. J. Human-Computer Studies, vol. 72, 2014, pp. 367–382.

[13] K. Muhammad, A. Lawlor, R. Rafter, and B. Smyth, "Great explanations: Opinionated explanations for recommendations," in Procs. of the 23rd International Conference on Case-Based Reasoning, E. Hüllermeier and M. Minor, Eds. Springer, 2015, pp. 244–258.

[14] S. Chang, F. M. Harper, and L. G. Terveen, "Crowd-based personalized natural language explanations for recommendations," in Procs. of the 10th ACM Conference on Recommender Systems. ACM, 2016, pp. 175–182.

[15] P. Symeonidis, A. Nanopoulos, and Y. Manolopoulos, "Moviexplain: A recommender system with explanations," in Procs. of the Third ACM Conference on Recommender Systems. ACM, 2009, pp. 317–320.

[16] M. Bilgic and R. Mooney, "Explaining recommendations: Satisfaction vs. promotion," in Procs. of Beyond Personalization: A Workshop on the Next Stage of Recommender Systems Research at the International Conference on Intelligent User Interfaces, 2005, pp. 13–18.

Recommender Systems for Spoken Word Radio

A Research-in-Progress of Requirements and Solutions

Stefan Hirschmeier, Roman Tilly, Detlef Schoder
Department of Information Systems and Information Management
University of Cologne
Cologne, Germany
email: {hirschmeier, tilly, schoder}@wim.uni-koeln.de

***Abstract*—The radio broadcasting industry had less innovation pressure compared to the music industry over the last years. But in the meantime, broadcasting agencies are increasingly competing with new music streaming services for listeners' limited attention and time. Radio broadcasting agencies react by building up personalized radio next to their linear playout, but have to face the difficulty that spoken word radio recommendation is more complex than music recommendation due to the heterogeneity of contents. We depict the requirements for radio recommendation, present the current data situation of broadcasters and a rough sketch of an architecture for a radio recommender system.**

Keywords—radio recommender system; radio broadcasting; individualized radio; non-linear radio; interstate broadcasting agreement

I. INTRODUCTION

Recommender Systems are on their way to enter a wide field of applications, and now also reach industries that had less innovation pressure in the last years, such as the radio broadcasting industry. Radio broadcasters are currently facing the challenge to build up a personalized experience for mobile radio on smartphones, next to their traditional linear program which comes out of the kitchen radio.

Radio broadcasters have their traditional business model and for many years did not feel much pressure to innovate. But in the meantime, broadcasting agencies are increasingly competing with new music streaming services for listeners' limited attention and time. Spotify had 100 million active users in mid 2016 [1] and 40 million subscribers in September 2016 [2] and is the market leader for music streaming services in many countries. As the music and film industry made significant advances, the radio broadcasting industry also more and more feels the pressure to innovate. Increasing music consumption might drain listeners from radio consumption, as time and attention of listeners are limited. Music and radio may find themselves competing for the attention of the same listeners. Radio broadcasters react by creating new channels to distribute their content, and one of the most promising new ways to bring content to users is a personalized radio experience on smartphones. Furthermore, personalized playlists have already become an expected standard for the younger generation, and the usage patterns that music and video streaming services established will very likely be expected of radio apps as well. Some broadcasters fear that if they do not manage to serve these usage patterns and keep up with state-of-the-art digital products, a generation tear-off might take place and broadcast organization will lose certain segments of listeners.

Especially recommender systems will become an important part of a radio broadcaster's new digital strategy. Few radio broadcasters like the U.S. National Public Radio (NPR) have already made advancements in the area of designing radio specific recommender systems and personalized radio.

Although radio broadcasting is a billion-euro-industry (134 billion US$ revenues of the U.S. broadcasting industry in 2014) [3][4] and reaches from 60 up to 90 percent of the population of all ages [5], there has been surprisingly little research on radio recommender systems.

The contribution of this paper is threefold: first, we present the most relevant requirements with respect to radio recommender systems; second, we present the current situation in broadcasting agencies, and third, we depict a generic solution approach for radio recommender systems.

The remainder of this paper is structured as follows: In the next Section, we resume on related work. In Section 3, we depict the requirements we elicited with focus on recommender systems for radio and the current data situation of broadcasters in Section 4. We present an appropriate solution design in Section 5. We follow up with a discussion and limitations in Section 6 and conclude with future research.

II. RELATED WORK

Not much research has been done on radio recommender systems. Hirschmeier et al. state challenges of radio recommendation in contrast to music recommendation [6]. Publications about radio recommendation sometimes cover music recommendation only, e.g., [7]–[12], as the term radio is also frequently used for pure music streaming services. Focusing on radio in terms of spoken work, Liu et al. [13] propose an approach about recommender systems that suggest which linear radio channel to switch to in the car. Also Moling et al. propose a client side recommender system that suggests which radio channel to switch to [14].

In this work, however, we focus on radio recommendation in terms of a non-linear playout of spoken word radio content.

Xie et al. [15] propose a mobile application that allows users to listen to personalized radio with focus on news. Casagranda et al. propose a hybrid content radio [16], enhancing the traditional broadcast radio experience and augmenting it with context-aware and personalized audio content from the internet, considering context like the listener's emotional state and activity, geographical position, and weather.

Schatter and Zeller [17] research on radio recommender systems with the focus on Digital Audio Broadcasting (DAB). Ala-Fossi et al. [18] and Anderson [19] also present studies about future delivery technologies of radio, but without placing a lot of emphasis on personalized content.

Considering radio program management, the book of Eastman and Ferguson presents an in-depth view on media programming [20]. Keith [21] specifically outlines program management for radio purposes.

III. Requirements for Radio Recommender Systems

In the following, we sum up the requirements that we elicited over the last months in discussions with representatives of broadcasting agencies, from presentations and talks, and from published articles. All requirements presented have a specific impact on the design of recommender systems for radio broadcasting. We however neglect all requirements that deal with the user interface and the appearance of personalized radio.

R1. Radio recommender systems need to reflect that radio is a mix of diverse contents

Radio is a mixture of diverse formats, such as news, talks, interviews, stories, radio plays, audio dramas, concerts, biographies, and long features. In contrast to music recommendation, where pieces are mainly characterized by a genre and an interpreter, radio pieces are much more multifaceted [6]. Apart from the diversification in formats, we also find diversification in topics (sports, music, politics, science, etc.), topicality (news vs. timeless content), depth with regard to content (funny, serious, in-depth, etc.), and duration (from less than a minute to more than one hour).

A radio recommender system has to cope with this diversity of content. Also, practitioners have the requirement that subgroups of content have their own recommendation technique or, at least learn the user's behaviour independent from each other. A user not interested in biographies of musicians might well be interested in other content about music. The diversity of radio content therefore feeds the assumption that groups of contents should be built, each having their own recommendation algorithms.

R2. Personalized radio also needs program management

In traditional radio, editors assemble the sequence of radio content, and over the years have built up personal or organizational knowledge how to assemble a good radio program. The program management of traditional radio is reflected in several levels: First, the broadcast schedule determines, which radio shows are being sent early in the morning, which ones in the evening, and on which day. It is the macro level structure of radio shows throughout the week and typically does not change a lot over time. Second, every hour in the week has a special clock – the broadcast clock – which is a template of contents being sent. The hour from Friday 3 pm to 4 pm, e.g., may start with a 3 minute newscast, continue with a 30 seconds music bed, then radio show segment A for 13 minutes, followed by an optional music bed for 2 minutes, radio show segment B, etc. Third, every show has its own clock and templates which editors use to structure their radio show.

The broadcast schedule at the macro level reflects what editors believe what suits their target group best, like a breakfast radio show in the morning or a newscast every full hour. On the other hand, the broadcast schedule represents a fixed timetable that listeners might integrate into their daily routine, so they know they can turn on the radio every morning at 7 am for their favorite radio show. Apart from the macro level program management, the micro level program management determines the contributions within a show. Radio editors decide from show to show, which contributions to send, and in which order. Radio editors have a certain feeling of how to assemble the parts of their radio show, and how to make the show enjoyable.

Assumably, the program management is one of the major factors what makes radio radio. Therefore, program management has to be reflected in personalized radio as well. Radio programming denotes the processes of selecting, scheduling, promoting and evaluating programs, and it does not matter, whether the programmer is a paid employee or the user [20]. Whereas in linear radio, the program management has been done by editors only, in personalized radio, the programming shifts to a multi-component issue, where three acting parties are involved: Editors, users, and algorithms. Whereas editors choose, which content is available for listening, recommender algorithms assemble a personalized selection and sequence of contents, and users give their input that makes the algorithms improve the playouts. Whereas users take over part of the programming, they still expect a ready-to-consume playlist, as Eastman and Ferguson state: "Viewers tend to choose channels and websites, but expect someone else to have filled those channels/sites in an expert way" [20].

R3. Interstate broadcasting treaties bring in special requirements

Considering personalized radio experiences, radio broadcasters have diverse objectives, depending on their mission and their funding. The question arises what determines the target function of a recommender system for radio.

"The main function of commercial media is to deliver an audience to advertisers" [20] one might say. In this regard, recommender systems help building exact profiles of listeners in order to keep them as long as possible engaged with digital products and to present them relevant advertisements. This is however not the target function of all radio broadcasters, especially not of publicly financed broadcasters. Those see their target function written down in the interstate broadcast agreement, usually referring to a formation of mature opinions of the public and balanced reporting. Whereas maximizing the length of stay on a digital product and maximizing the revenues from a listener's engagement seems a straight-forward goal for recommender systems, the normative influence of interstate broadcasting agreements on personalized playouts needs to be reflected in radio recommender systems as well.

With these objectives in mind, personalized radio faces a specific filter bubble challenge. Personalized radio may easily end up with users being trapped in an echo chamber, contradicting with the ideas of a public radio. As a consequence, radio broadcasters need to have special control over the program composing algorithms that assemble the personalized sequence of radio contents. The resulting sequence should therefore not only be a mix of recommended items, but also include externally induced items, allowing for serendipity and a wider horizon.

R4. Context-sensitivity

Whereas the previous requirements bear the intention to hold on to the characteristics of linear radio and transfer them to personalized radio, context sensitivity supports the idea to make personalized radio a richer experience than linear radio. As of today, only time of day and day of week can be reflected in the linear radio program. For mobile radio, more context factors are relevant like location, habits of the user, surrounding noise, surrounding light, activity, movement, temperature, weather, availability of bandwidth, output device, and other context parameters. Context-sensitivity may therefore influence both which content is played and in which sequence. A rich context-sensitivity is still more on the wish list of broadcasting agencies than on the requirements list. But broadcasters will move towards the goal to provide their personalized listening experience in a sophisticated, context-sensitive way.

IV. Data Situation of Radio Broadcasters

Current technical infrastructures of radio broadcasters are optimized for linear distribution of the content. These systems have not been designed to bring rich metadata along with the content. Typically, at the time when content goes on air for linear distribution, only few to none metadata about radio shows is available. Figure 1 shows the availability of metadata along the lifecycle of radio content in a typical scenario. Even if metadata is generated afterwards, e.g., for enriching the digital representation of content on the website or for archiving purposes, the dominance of linear distribution structures complicates the provisioning of digital content on websites, media centers, and especially for recommender systems. Whereas few broadcasters have already overthought their metadata generating processes, the situation depicted in Figure 1 still holds for many broadcasting agencies.

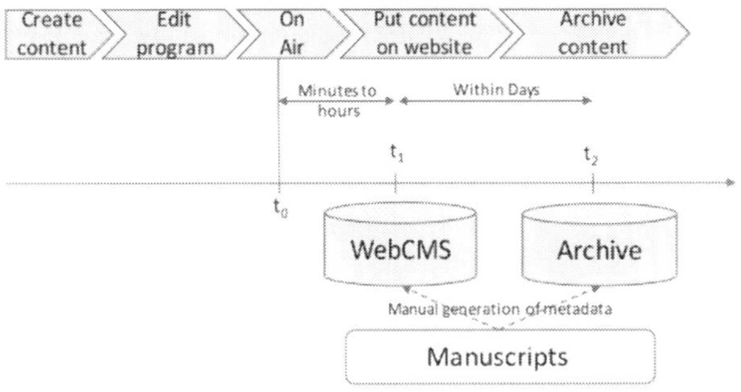

Figure 1. Availability of metadata along the lifecycle of content

The non-availability of metadata has two major implications: First, radio broadcasters will most likely focus on collaborative filtering techniques when initially building up a recommender system, and second, if they want to enrich the personalized listening experience with content-based recommendation approaches, they need to change processes, organization, and technical infrastructure accordingly, so metadata will be available in time.

V. Solution Approach

In the following, we present a generic architecture for radio recommender systems that match the requirements presented before. The architecture also reflects experiences that have already been made by innovative broadcasters that force the development of recommender systems.

The generic architecture foresees the division of all radio content into several groups. Each of these groups has its own recommendation algorithms and may also incorporate context information. Next to content groups, for which recommender algorithms are applied, there is also content which should be kept out of the recommender system, e.g., news. A program composer component assembles a personalized playout in the end. Figure 2 depicts the generic architecture.

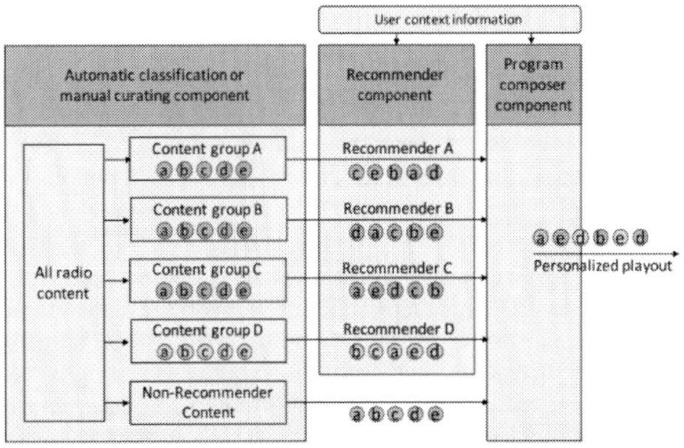

Figure 2. A generic architecture for radio recommender systems

A. A recommender algorithm for each content group

To meet requirement R1, all radio content should be subdivided into homogeneous groups. It is the broadcaster's decision which and how many groups to build. This decision, how many and which groups of content to build, and which recommender algorithms to implement, may well differ according to the needs and the orientation of the broadcaster and to the individual understanding what makes a good program.

Experiments have shown that with respect to listening satisfaction, recommender with curating outperforms recommendation alone. That is, the content is manually curated into groups (e.g., lead stories, core stories, break stories and invest stories, in the case of NPR [22]), and each group has its own recommendation technique.

B. *A separate program composer component*

To meet requirement R2, a separate program composer component exists that enables a sophisticated program management. The program composer algorithm, which defines the individual radio program sequence, then assembles the personalized radio program according to broadcaster-specific rules or patterns. In this program sequence, also non-recommender content such as newscast can be embedded. This way, the broadcaster not only maintains full control over how to assemble the recommended items from each content group, but also over the integration of content that prevents the user get into a filter bubble, in order to meet requirement R3.

As of current research, BBC Research & Development puts efforts in understanding what makes a good mix, and how to put this into templates or algorithms [23].

C. *Context awareness for both recommender algorithms and the composer component*

To meet requirement R4, context information may both influence the recommender algorithms and the program composer component. Ideally, context factors are already reflected in the recommender algorithms. But as the context of the user might change unexpectedly, the program composer component might adapt to the changed context much quicker, as it is the final sequence generator. Also for non-recommender content, the program composer can make use of context information.

Whereas a lot of knowledge about content-aware recommender systems already exists [24], more research has to be done specifically for the spoken word radio domain. The same holds for the architecture presented in general; it is still generic, as we still lack research results in detail.

VI. Discussion and Future Research

The requirements, situations and solution approaches depicted in this paper represent our view on the status quo of recommender systems in the radio broadcasting industry. Both requirements and solution approaches might still develop, as recommender systems for radio are just emerging and our perspective might not be all-embracing. More research has to be done on the questions what makes up a good radio program, and how to incorporate this into algorithms. The answers to these questions will presumably be case-centric, as every broadcaster might find an individual solution depending on their specific profile. The insight about the ingredients for a good program in turn determines which groups of contents to build before the recommendation takes place. Especially for publicly funded radio broadcasters, the question arises how exactly the influence of the interstate broadcast agreements should be shaped.

Further, practitioners and researchers have to think about the feedback channel of radio recommender systems. Whereas the feedback channel of the user's interactions is crucial for every recommender system in order to iteratively improve on the recommendation quality, in radio recommender systems the feedback goes far beyond the pure algorithmic improvement – it reaches back to the sphere of activities of the editors and producers. In other words, radio recommender systems should inform the editors and producers which content to produce more/less, how to improve meta-data, and how recommendations were taken up by listeners, i.e., gauge effectiveness of the recommendation algorithms. The feedback could also include explicit questions and comments from the consumers voiced through a mobile app.

Thus, radio recommendation should not be considered as a unidirectional communication like traditional radio – from producer to consumer – but as the possibility to enable the interaction of producer and consumer with respect to content.

References

[1] Spotify, "Number of global monthly active Spotify users from July 2012 to June 2016," 2016: https://www.statista.com/statistics/367739/spotify-global-mau/. [Accessed: 30-Jan-2017].

[2] VentureBeat, "Number of paying Spotify subscribers worldwide from July 2010 to September 2016," 2016: https://www.statista.com/statistics/244995/number-of-paying-spotify-subscribers/. [Accessed: 30-Jan-2017].

[3] US Census Bureau, "Estimated expenses of the U.S. broadcasting industry from 2007 to 2014," 2014: https://www.statista.com/statistics/185403/estimated-expenses-of-the-us-broadcasting-industry-since-2005/. [Accessed: 30-Jan-2017].

[4] Ofcom, "International Communications Market Report," 2015: https://www.ofcom.org.uk/__data/assets/pdf_file/0020/31268/icmr_2015.pdf. [Accessed: 30-Jan-2017].

[5] IfD Allensbach, "Population in Germany per frequency of radio consumption in the years 2012 to 2016," 2016: https://de.statista.com/statistik/daten/studie/170993/umfrage/haeufigkeit-von-radiohoeren/. [Accessed: 30-Jan-2017].

[6] S. Hirschmeier, D. A. Döppner, and D. Schoder, "Stating and Discussing Challenges of Radio Recommender Systems in Contrast to Music Recommendation," in *Proceedings of the 2nd International Workshop on Decision Making and Recommender Systems*, Bozen Bolzano, 2015.

[7] V. Zaharchuk, D. I. Ignatov, A. Konstantinov, and S. Nikolenko, "A New Recommender System for the Interactive Radio Network FMhost," Jan. 2012.

[8] F. V. Hecht, T. Bocek, N. Bär, R. Erdin, B. Kuster, M. Zeeshan, and B. Stiller, "Radiommender: P2P on-line radio with a distributed recommender system," in *IEEE 12th International Conference on Peer-to-Peer Computing*, 2012.

[9] C. Hayes and P. Cunningham, "Smart radio — community based music radio," *Knowledge-Based Systems*, vol. 14, no. 3–4, pp. 197–201, Jun. 2001.

[10] G. Dziczkowski, L. Bougueroua, and K. Wegrzyn-Wolska, "Social Network - An Autonomous System Designed for Radio Recommendation," in *2009 International Conference on Computational Aspects of Social Networks*, 2009, pp. 57–64.

[11] D. I. Ignatov, S. I. Nikolenko, T. Abaev, and J. Poelmans, "Online recommender system for radio station hosting based on information fusion and adaptive tag-aware profiling," *Expert Systems with Applications*, vol. 55, pp. 546–558, Aug. 2016.

[12] D. R. Turnbull, J. A. Zupnick, K. B. Stensland, A. R. Horwitz, A. J. Wolf, A. E. Spirgel, S. P. Meyerhofer, and T. Joachims, "Using Personalized Radio to Enhance Local Music Discovery," in *CHI '14 Extended Abstracts on Human Factors in Computing Systems*, New York, 2014, pp. 2023–2028.

[13] N.-H. Liu, "Design of an Intelligent Car Radio and Music Player System," *Multimedia Tools and Applications*, vol. 72, no. 2, pp. 1341–1361, Sep. 2014.

[14] O. Moling, L. Baltrunas, and F. Ricci, "Optimal Radio Channel Recommendations with Explicit and Implicit Feedback," in *Proceedings of the Sixth ACM Conference on Recommender Systems*, New York, 2012, pp. 75–82.

[15] Y. Xie, L. Chen, K. Jia, L. Ji, and J. Wu, "iNewsBox: Modeling and Exploiting Implicit Feedback for Building Personalized News Radio," in *Proceedings of the 22nd ACM International Conference on Information & Knowledge Management*, New York, 2013, pp. 2485–2488.

[16] P. Casagranda, A. Erk, S. O'Halpin, D. Born, and W. Huijten, "A framework for a context-based hybrid content radio," in *The best of the IET and IBC*, 2015, pp. 41–47.

[17] G. Schatter and B. Zeller, "Design and Implementation of an Adaptive Digital Radio DAB using Content Personalization on the Basis of Standards," *IEEE Transactions on Consumer Electronics*, vol. 53, no. 4, pp. 1353–1361, Nov. 2007.

[18] M. Ala-Fossi, S. Lax, B. O'Neill, P. Jauert, and H. Shaw, "The Future of Radio is Still Digital—But Which One? Expert Perspectives and Future Scenarios for Radio Media in 2015," *Journal of Radio & Audio Media*, vol. 15, no. 1, pp. 4–25, Mai 2008.

[19] J. N. Anderson, "Radio broadcasting's digital dilemma," *Convergence: International Journal of Research into New Media Technologies*, Sep. 2012.

[20] S. T. Eastman and D. A. Ferguson, *Media Programming: Strategies and Practices*. Wadsworth Publishing, 2012.

[21] M. C. Keith, *The Radio Station*, 8th ed. Focal Press, 2012.

[22] Z. Brand, "NPR Digital Media: lessons learned in creating and delivering a digital listening experience," presented at the Radio 2.0 Keynote, Paris, 2015: http://de.slideshare.net/NicolasMoulard/npr-digital-media-lessons-learned-in-creating-and-delivering-a-digital-listening-experience-radio-20-2015. [Accessed: 02-Feb-2017].

[23] K. Sommers, "Understanding Editorial Decisions," *BBC Research & Development*, 06-Feb-2016: http://www.bbc.co.uk/rd/blog/2016-05-understanding-editorial-decisions. [Accessed: 02-Feb-2017].

[24] F. Ricci, L. Rokach, and B. Shapira, Eds., *Recommender Systems Handbook*. Springer, 2015.